Organizational Justice and Organizational Change

Although various factors contribute to failed change, one of the key reasons for change failure is the inability of leaders to gain the trust of employees, to understand the interaction between their subordinates, and to convince them to support change and to commit the energy and effort necessary to implement it.

The aims of this book are to establish theories in order to describe and explain how human behaviors and contexts interact dynamically in these changes, and manage change and justice by reducing inequalities, giving emphasis to distributive justice. In addition, the aim of this book is also for readers to better understand employees' perceptions of organizational justice by senior management which is particularly important during the organizational change because change cannot succeed without the acceptance and support from employees. *Organizational Justice and Organizational Change: Managing by Love* provides readers a theoretical understanding and recommendations for acting properly in an organization, forming a comprehensive tool and better enable practitioners to achieve management of change and justice in organizations.

It will be of interest to researchers, academics, practitioners, and students in the fields of change management, organizational studies, leadership, and strategic management.

Dominique A. David is a distinguished senior manager, multidisciplinary researcher, published author, and consultant specialized in restructuring businesses, including bankruptcies cases.

Routledge Focus on Business and Management

The fields of business and management have grown exponentially as areas of research and education. This growth presents challenges for readers trying to keep up with the latest important insights. Routledge Focus on Business and Management presents small books on big topics and how they intersect with the world of business research.

Individually, each title in the series provides coverage of a key academic topic, whilst collectively, the series forms a comprehensive collection across the business disciplines.

Global Entrepreneurship Analytics
Using GEM Data
Milenka Linneth Argote Cusi and León Darío Parra Bernal

The Customer Experience Model
Adyl Aliekperov

Organizational Justice and Organizational Change
Managing by Love
Dominique A. David

Cultural Proximity and Organization
Managing Diversity and Innovation
Federica Ceci and Francesca Masciarelli

For more information about this series, please visit: www.routledge.com/Routledge-Focus-on-Business-and-Management/book-series/FBM

Organizational Justice and Organizational Change

Managing by Love

Dominique A. David

NEW YORK AND LONDON

First published 2021
by Routledge
605 Third Avenue, New York, NY 10017

and by Routledge
2 Park Square, Milton Park, Abingdon, Oxon, OX14 4RN

First issued in paperback 2022

Routledge is an imprint of the Taylor & Francis Group, an informa business

Publisher's Note
The publisher has gone to great lengths to ensure the quality of this reprint but points out that some imperfections in the original copies may be apparent.

Library of Congress Cataloging-in-Publication Data
Names: David, Dominique A., author.
Title: Organizational justice and organizational change: managing by love / Dominique A. David.
Description: New York, NY: Routledge, 2021. | Series: Routledge focus on business and management | Includes bibliographical references and index.
Identifiers: LCCN 2020019639 | ISBN 9780367857967 (hbk) | ISBN 9781003057659 (ebk)
Subjects: LCSH: Organizational change–Management. | Leadership. | Equality.
Classification: LCC HD58.8 .D364 2021 | DDC 658.4/06–dc23
LC record available at https://lccn.loc.gov/2020019639

ISBN: 978-0-367-52378-7 (pbk)
ISBN: 978-0-367-85796-7 (hbk)
ISBN: 978-1-003-05765-9 (ebk)

DOI: 10.4324/9781003057659

Typeset in Times New Roman
by Deanta Global Publishing Services, Chennai, India

Beyond Gödel's recommendation, facing new theory, the most important thing is to know what one can do concretely with it—without forgetting the following canonical words: vanity of vanities, and all is vanity.

Contents

Figures

Tables

About the Author

Dominique A. David DBA is a distinguished senior manager, multidisciplinary researcher, published author, and consultant specialized in restructuring businesses including bankruptcies cases. His scientific education is rooted mostly in computer sciences, economics, and business administration.

As a young French state commercial engineer in computer sciences, he started marketing computer peripherals with CDME, a wholly owned subsidiary of Lebon Industry, which was the company that brought gas light in Paris. Then, he spent more than ten years in the marketing of hand-held computers worldwide, working at the beginning with MSI Data Corporation, which won the President "E" award US Trade Export, before introducing to Europe with SISIG, the first pocket computer equipped with a tactile screen made in Japan by Canon Inc. During another decade he worked in partnership with Fidal (KPMG Peat Marwick) for restructuring businesses in France, mostly in the IT industry, while still working closely with AID3 Group to promote a multi task real-time objects oriented electronic architecture for mobile phones that is considered today as the pioneer of the iPhone. Doing business in more than 40 countries as a C-level executive or business consultant, while benefiting from learning advanced know-how in management with firms like Clinvest (Crédit Lyonnais) or Franchise Services Inc., he promoted advanced technologies in various industrial sectors and gained expertise in managing corporate turnaround or high growth businesses including M&A or strategic alliances.

Currently, he is in charge of promoting a disruptive IT concept worldwide, moving human intelligence and knowledge into a new paradigm, while leading the technical commission of Cercle de Réflexion des Nations (CRN) for promoting *human duties* at the UN General Assembly in New York.

Dr. David has been recently admitted in the Gazarian promotion of the Doctorate of Peace Administration at UNCR University, Florida, USA, while pursuing a PhD in Sociology at the University of Tunis in memory of Ibn Khaldoun, and a PhD in Instructional Design and Online Learning at Euclid University, Bangui, CAR.

Part I

Problematic, Concepts and Context

1 Problematic

Problem Statement

Considering that it is crucial for developing theories allowing organizations to get practical outcomes during periods of change, scholars call for a more dynamic conceptualization of organizational justice (OJ) in the workplace, and a better understanding of perceptions of justice during organizational change (OC) processes. The problem is that despite the many theories, implementation strategies, and approaches, successful OC remains elusive, which may explain the poor success rate of change programs in general. Change initiatives are among the most important projects an organization can undertake as successful outcomes could bring competitive advantages, while failure could have catastrophic consequences.

Organizational scholars contend that employees will assume a positive approach to OC if they perceive their treatment by management and the organization as being fair. Most scholars argue that employees' perceptions of trust and fairness impact the success of change initiatives, while others advocate more broadly that OJ is key to succeeding in any OC. Nevertheless, perceptions of justice like OJ or managers' perceptions of justice (MPJ) depend on norms of justice, their interpretations, and the willingness to act according to rules that these norms suggest to people within contexts that change over time. Furthermore, due to the dynamics and complexity of social exchanges, some authors state that economics and management theories could profit from a clearer understanding of shared norms. Thus, an opportunity exists for investigating and documenting a deeper understanding of how and why perceptions of justice interact during change in organizations. Therefore, the rationale and foundational elements of this theoretical essay include the need for a new theoretical understanding allowing organizations to achieve practical outcomes during periods of change.

Questions

Aligning with the above Problem Statement, a central question (CQ) is developed: How are norms of justice, perceptions of these norms, and decisions related to these perceptions interwoven when people assess change and justice in organizations? Regarding the framework's components of a research design (i.e., epistemology, theoretical perspective, methodology, and method), Creswell (2003) explained how three elements of inquiry (i.e., knowledge claims, strategies, and methods) combine to form different approaches to research, and help determine how to collect and analyze data. Thus, social constructivism combined with interpretivism and pragmatism define together the overall approach of this theoretical essay, which allows the researcher to be free to choose methods, techniques, and procedures of research that best meet their needs and purposes. Therefore, and in line with the CQ, two sub-research questions (SQs) are developed:

SQ1: How can OJ be improved during OC?
SQ2: How do contexts and behaviors interact while change takes place?

Purpose of the Essay

The purpose of this theoretical essay is twofold:

1) First, to introduce the Paradox of Fairness that results from a non-egalitarian paradigm, in order to gain a better understanding of the interactions among OJ, employees' perceptions of justice (EPJ), and MPJ during OC, while providing new concepts (e.g., Point of Origin).
2) Second, to provide some recommendations toward establishing a general theory to describe and explain how human behaviors and contexts interact dynamically (i.e., the development and operation of social constructs in organizations).

Nature of the Essay

The nature of this theoretical essay is qualitative. The essay utilizes an inductive top-down method of theorizing using the results of an integrated literature review method. This theoretical essay is founded on the nature of behaviors that drive individuals toward pursuits in social action, as participants in activities pertaining to whatever they may have had reason to value. People engaged in social action provide a philosophical framework for a grounded theory essay. The substantive exploration of behaviors, grounded in empirical data, guided this investigation of how people and processes influence people to produce social actions.

This essay is presented in a way that provides the reader with certain progress in the analysis of data to the theoretical construction. The integrated literature review maps the scope of this essay and provides a framework for the boundaries of what the essay includes, as well as the limiting factors for what it does not. The integrated literature review offers a meaningful raw material in its groundwork for the methodology chapter.

Research Objectives/Sub-Problems Related to the Problem Statement

Research objectives and sub-problems of the Problem Statement are divided into two steps, with the aim of facilitating inquiries relatively to each research question. First, the objective is to examine how norms of justice, perceptions of these norms, and decisions related to these perceptions are interwoven when people assess change and justice in organizations. The fact that interactions between norms and perceptions of justice are part of decision making for assessments of justice (e.g., fairness), leads to examining how change interacts in this decision making. Moreover, because change occurs over time, for data analysis to be justifiable (i.e., transparent, coherent, and communicable), there is a theoretical need to advance understanding on how contexts and behaviors interact. Thus, one needs to examine why norms of justice, perceptions of these norms, and decisions related to these perceptions are interleaved when people assess change and justice in organizations. The fact that the emotional part of a perception (i.e., sensation) is a non-linear process, while verbal expression of a perception follows a linear logic, leads to the question of meaning in contexts. Therefore, this double interpretation (self-sensation and choice of words), which depends on gender and on cultural environments, needs to be addressed for the robustness of the essay.

Second, having analyzed the data collected from the literature, one must get a better understanding of how and why norms, perceptions, and decisions are related when people assess change or justice. Therefore, the author investigated how the interactions between OJ and MPJ facilitate OC management. This latest objective of this theoretical essay will be fulfilled by examining to what extent OC failures originate from: faulty norms of justice; employees' or managers' faulty perceptions of justice; or faulty decision-making when managing change or justice in organizations.

Significance of the Essay

Theoretical Contribution

Due to the fact that the non-egalitarian paradigm suggested by the author has been mostly neglected, this *selbstverblendung* (i.e., incomprehensible blindness) has huge consequences for any human organizational theory.

The Paradox of Fairness improves understanding of managing change and justice in organizations. The Point of Origin, the Affordances of Contexts, and the appropriate use of a Restricted Deontic Logic (RDL) (i.e., ternary logic) together provide a new theoretical framework and a new orientation for scholars to do further research toward establishing a general theory to describe and better explain how behaviors and contexts interact dynamically.

Practical Contribution

Taking all the above into consideration (i.e., held in mind) improves understanding of how to implement at best distributive justice in private or public organizations—which in practice improves the chances to succeed with any OC process.

Limitations of the Essay

The non-egalitarian paradigm shift that needs to be done meets resistance due to the habits of human beings regarding the shared norms currently related to equality conventions.

Delimitations of the Essay

The main delimitation is that the literature has been voluntarily restricted (i.e., filtered), and consequently it doesn't take into account all human knowledge regarding the phenomenon under investigation.

Bibliography

Creswell, J. W. (2003). *Research design: Qualitative, quantitative, and mixed method approaches*. Thousand Oaks, CA: Sage Publications.

2 Concepts

Theoretical Prolegomena

Theorem of Uniqueness

There are words that carry a lot of emotions—like *love* and *freedom*—*justice* is one of them. The intelligence of human beings is a mix of emotional intelligence and verbal intelligence. Emotional intelligence develops first, then comes language, and verbal intelligence constructs itself on and with emotions. Emotions come from our senses. They are the basic means by which we discover our context (i.e., environment we are in). At the beginning, this context is analyzed through a primary mechanism of categorization (PCM) based on pleasure/displeasure (Fidaali, 1987). Each human being travels across many environments during his or her life, facing multiple experiments, which constitute individually our emotional and verbal experiences. The latter help, through language, to experiment virtually with environments we are in or out. All are more or less rituals in sense-making to provide some sense-giving of human life. Each of us is a result of at least a meeting of two human beings (i.e., male and female). With in-vitro technicality, such reproduction can be reduced to one female. Whatever the modality for insemination, that female is not alone, and she is part of the newborn context. Therefore, since the time of being in the uterus, PCM occurs and helps each of us to construct our first emotional landmarks. All emotional and verbal experiences are more or less perceived, which constitute a unique background that contributes to determining our traits (e.g., ego). This uniqueness is not the appanage of human beings but of each living being, and beyond is valid for everything. Therefore, even the equals sign (i.e., =) is a powerful invention/convention (i.e., a shared norm) for human societies; with no doubt, we can write the following postulate:

$$\forall x, \forall y, \neg (x = y)$$

which is a conjecture always true within a space-time, that can be symbolically reformulated more intuitively as follows:

$$\forall x, \nexists y \,/\, x = y$$

Whatever x, there is no y, as $x = y$; equality doesn't exist (i.e., = is always false) in the real life of human beings. The concept of equality (i.e., =) as a language tool, is a simplifying artefact of human thought, which is useful for calculus but a non-sense when applying in the real world. In other words, traditional social equality posture enhances inequality across human beings. The only way to reduce inequality is to treat each human being differently—there is no other way. This is what I call the Paradox of Fairness: to be equitable (i.e., to be fair), one has to behave unequally vis-à-vis people. Thus, resulting from the Theorem of Uniqueness, asymmetry rules the world and one can conceive that a non-egalitarian paradigm in which the Paradox of Fairness is true has huge consequences (e.g., social and political) for human organizations. Moreover, although life is a continuous process, due to our limitations, the perceptions of different situations are often non-linear, which leads to the consciousness concept of change.

Change

Change is a double process. There are two categories of change, both of which explain that for organizational scholars the word *complexity* is most often associated with this concept. One is a change that happens in context. This change is a non-stop process, because the environment always varies. The other change is due to the fact that the observer that I am changes itself over time. Moreover, these double changes intertwine over time, providing infinite variations of realities (i.e., perceptions of the environment) within a lot of ambiguities that need to be managed. Although it is impossible to account for all of these realities, it is nevertheless possible to conceive why and how they are produced and why and how human beings select some of them (i.e., the disambiguation mechanisms), and then look at what they do with them. Such an approach helps to better understand (i.e., to construct shared meanings) why and how people behave (i.e., causality behavior), and particularly what are the reasons for (e.g., interest)—i.e., why—and what are the ways of (e.g., intention, volition)—i.e., how one person behaves with another (i.e., managing *attention* using communication means) in order to achieve various goals of doing something or not with others (e.g., playing, working, fighting, etc.), which is sometimes done just for enhancing the self-experimentation of PCM one more time. While most human experience (e.g., verbal or emotional) reinforces the system of hierarchies and others the basic principles of group living (e.g., motivation for and benefit of), copying from naturalistic observations, some human constructs (e.g., organizations) help to navigate planned or unplanned asymmetries of change (i.e., living with the uncertainty of everyday life).

Organization

In everyday life, building communication means is a must as soon as we are not alone. That is why language exists. The languages across human beings are more or less rich in symbols (e.g., words and signs) with a variety of meanings (i.e., interpretations). All often vary (i.e., change) according to environmental characteristics that we have invented as landmarks (e.g., scale, location, time, etc.), while increasing the precision and complexity of our thoughts (i.e., human knowledge). When two persons meet, a process begins. Each is going to progressively discover what to do or not do with the other. According to their differences or resemblances, this is a multiform process using the communication means of each person in order to build with the other what people call a relationship. In fact, multiple relations are simultaneously undertaken, and some connections that are made are more useful to bridge, and then reinforce what they are or are not doing together.

These relations are the basic unit of analysis for any organizational perspective, because they are the roots of a social construct (i.e., more than one), called social capital, which is more or less defined by shared norms. Then, defining an organization is a matter of boundaries (i.e., who is included) and contents (i.e., for what purpose). Organizational and social exchanges start with two people (i.e., more than one), and expand progressively according to the boundaries decided on, most of the time by these first "promoters". Then, a third person comes along, and triadic substitutes to dyadic relationships open up new opportunities (e.g., behavioral game) for the nascent group forming the root of social capital (i.e., shared norms).

Human Rationality

Managing change and human rationality using shared norms are two inseparable concepts. The rationality of human beings is built for managing change permanently. Moreover, due that contexts and behaviors are changing constantly, interpretations change over time. Therefore, enhancing understanding of "understanding" and understanding of what "change" is, and how to manage both, is a central and strategic issue for organizations ruled by economic principles.

Instead of characterizing human beings by their willingness to navigate between *destiny* and *providence*, I do consider that both *destiny* and *providence* constitute the environments (i.e., a continuum of opportunities) in which human beings have to take decisions over time for acting (e.g., thinking). Like the theory of complex adaptive systems or the improvisation metaphor, or like some recent theoretical frameworks that use a combination of both to illuminate how an open-processional change model works, I agree that human beings or organizations have to build rationality for first learning how to survive within this continuum of opportunities and threats (i.e., continuous change of their environments), but I push forward an examination showing how the behaviors of ancient peoples did the same in order to dig out the underlying rules that explain such a common behavior's process. The result is to gain a more comprehensive view of the whole picture while providing insights for a possible generalization of how to manage change while obtaining acceptance (whatever the contexts).

From the author's perspective, human understanding is a verbal construction, which looks like a process more related to hermeneutics of acts than to the interpretation of a dialog. Using co-occurrence of interpretations of acts, and then making a choice that makes sense, constitutes human understanding. Such an approach is much closer to the principle of linguistic relativity (Whorf, 1956), or an extension of general relativity (Einstein, 1916), than simply application of the definition of intelligence coming from the theory of evolution (Darwin, 1871).

Furthermore, looking at how cells are dying when compared to stars helps to explain how the primary mechanism of cellular stress and the primary mechanism of human understanding (i.e., PCM) are both built in a systemic (Bertalanffy, 1968). Therefore, applying the concept of affordance (Gibson, 1979) to contexts while using Fields of Coherence (FoC) (Ravatin, 1992, 2008) ruled by a restricted deontic logic (RDL), all leads to the foundation of a new theory for describing and explaining how on a daily basis human rationality that produces behaviors works when facing various environments. Consequently, whatever the corpus used and the referent environment, closed or open, producing a "meaning" is not an autopoietic mechanism but an interactive process, despite the fact that at the end such meaning becomes arbitrarily something real or true for people, and from this point it behaves as a social autopoietic system itself built within a simple and basic determinism process (i.e., a symmetry breaking) regarding its conformity.

Context

Although change is a process of continual renewal, whatever the theoretical approach, three useful categories have been identified as change characterized by the rate of occurrence, by how it comes about, and by scale. Nevertheless, such descriptive categories do not help to explain how human beings are making decisions over time, and due to the rate of failure in implementing change—i.e., 70%—one can say there is a basic lack of a valid framework of how to successfully implement and manage OC, since what is currently available is a wide range of contradictory and confusing theories and approaches, which are mostly lacking empirical evidence and often based on unchallenged hypotheses regarding the nature of contemporary OC management. Whatsoever, this issue of change management is closely linked to the process of decision-making.

Decision-making seems to be something personal, a personal act, but in fact this act is always done according to a context. One cannot separate this act from the context in which it happens, regardless of the way one considers or characterizes this act (e.g., thinking or doing something else or nothing), and this basic process of acting of human beings is true whatever the environment is—open or closed.

For this reason, the unit of analysis of organizational studies ought to be one human being in his context. Therefore, throughout this book, each human being is considered as a Point of Origin of the context in which and from which he is taking basic decisions for acting. Each human being and his context attached constitute all together the unit of analysis under examination.

Key Terms

The definitions of terms that follow relate to unique terms used in the course of this theoretical essay.

Affordance

An affordance is a resource that the environment offers any animal that has the capabilities to perceive and use it. When used in this sense, the term affordance refers to the perceived and actual properties of the thing, primarily those fundamental properties that determine just how the thing could be used. A chair affords ("is for") support and, therefore, affords to sit.

Allopoiesis

Allopoiesis refers to the process whereby a system produces something other than the system itself.

Attention

Attention refers to the internal mechanism that determines the significance of stimuli and thereby makes it impossible to predict behavior by stimulus consideration alone. Attention is controllable (i.e., the organism appears to control the choice of stimuli that will be allowed, in turn to control its behavior) and selective (i.e., the organism selectively attends to some stimuli, or aspects of stimulation, in preference to others), which are functions that require an effort (Kahneman, 1973; Ocasio, 1997).

Autopoiesis

Autopoiesis refers to a system capable of reproducing and maintaining itself. Then, such a system has been adapted to organizations.

Change

From the author's perspective, change is a double process. There are two categories of change, both of which explain that the word "complexity" is most often associated with this concept. One is a change that happens in context. This change is a non-stop process because the environment always varies. The other change is due to the fact that the observer that I am changes itself over time.

Cognitive Bias

Cognitive bias refers to preconceived notions (e.g., a theorist's idiosyncratic knowledge of the literature) about what is important, which direct and focus attention. Thus, biases are developed as consequences of a theorist's own interest and prior knowledge.

Consciousness

Consciousness can be defined as a reflexive process: perceiving one's own perceptions.

Context

Context is a concept that refers to the surroundings associated with the phenomena, which help to illuminate those phenomena—typically factors associated with units of analysis above those expressly under investigation.

Creative Thinking

Critical and creative thought are both achievements of thought. Creativity masters a process of making or producing, criticality a process of assessing or judging. Creative achievements are the basis for progress in our world. Although creative achievement is influenced by many variables, the basis for creativity is held to lie in the generation of high-quality, original, and elegant solutions to complex, novel, ill-defined problems.

Critical Thinking

Critical thinking is a meta-cognitive process that, through purposeful and reflective judgment, increases the chances of producing a logical conclusion to an argument or solution to a problem. Instruction in critical thinking has become exceedingly important because it allows individuals to gain a more complex understanding of information they encounter and promotes good decision-making and problem-solving in real-world applications.

Deontic Logic

Deontic logic is a logical system that studies propositions and truth functions of propositions about obligatory, permitted, forbidden, and other derivative deontic characters of acts and performance functions of acts (Von Wright, 1968).

Disambiguation

Disambiguation is a process or a mean that allows one to make a choice vis-à-vis landmarks. Such a process or mean refers to the removal of ambiguity by making something clear. Word sense disambiguation is a technique to find the exact sense of an ambiguous word in a particular context (Pal & Saha, 2015).

Distributive Justice

On the basis of ethical and objective factors, this term describes the same treatment given to similar employees and different treatments for different employees (Wang, Liao, Xia, & Chang, 2010).

Environment

Environment can be defined as situational opportunities and constraints that affect the occurence and meaning of organizational behavior as well as functional relationships between variables.

Field of Coherence

This is the process that links sensory representation to conceptual representation (Shepherd & Sutcliffe, 2011). Such a process is ruled both by linear and non-linear logic.

Informational Justice

Informational justice refers to the justness as viewed by employees of the information utilized in making a decision.

Interpersonal Justice

Interpersonal justice reflects the thought given to the situations of people, and the civility, respect, and compassion exhibited for a person's feelings.

Landmarks

From the author's perspective, without landmarks one cannot act (e.g., thinking, moving), and the perception of landmarks should be part of a definition of consciousness.

Meanings

From the author's perspective, the ability of human beings to practice natural language and to manage meanings of words and texts, including ideas or concepts, whatever the abstraction used, constitutes what one commonly calls verbal intelligence.

Norms

Norms are a set of recommendations that are reinforced through the practice of people who agree to put in practice such recommendations (e.g., communities of practice are driven by shared norms). Norms have functions (e.g., social, quality, identity) that help to achieve either some expectations (e.g., individual or collective) or a well-identified goal (e.g., regulation, welfare, loyalty), all built within conditional preferences for following behavioral rules, which constitute social interactions.

Organizational Justice

Organizational justice describes the views of employees on the fairness of treatment within an organization.

Organizational Trust

Organizational trust refers to faith in the system, culture, and structure of the organization in which an employee works.

Perceptions

Perceptions are realities of the perceivers. Interpretations of these perceptions are decisions. Therefore, the study of perception is a bundle of the study of decision-making (i.e., cognition) that precedes any human behavior (Fearing, 1954).

Procedural Justice

Procedural justice is a term used to refer to the views of employees on the justness employed in the means and procedures used to control or manage a process.

Resistance to Change

This term describes an approach toward change as one not readily embracing it by those it affects, taking into account the cognitive, behavioral, and affective elements, rendering it a three-dimensional construct (e.g., employee motivation and resistance to organizational change).

Rules

From the author's perspective, rules are different from norms because a rule requires or prohibits behaviors (e.g., being a student means following some rules). Moreover, most of the time, there are sanctions attached to rules if they are not applied. This means that rules are often set up by a body (e.g., individuals or organizations such as states) having authority over those who have to follow the rules that have been set. By contrast, norms are often conventions that emerge from habits or behaviors coming from the bottom of the field, while rules are most of the time the result of a top-down process, including punishment for deviant behaviors.

Social Norms

Social norms are the rules and conventions that guide the conduct of members of a society: how we dress, what and how we eat, where and how we travel, our recreation, and the way we work. Social norms, like many other social phenomena, are the unplanned, unexpected result of individuals' interactions. It has been argued that social norms ought to be understood as a kind of grammar of social interactions.

Strategic Change

Strategic change has to do with an organizational change, transformational in nature, driven by top management with the goal of comprehensively changing the direction of the organization and significantly altering its original vision and business model.

Thinking

From the author's perspective, the act of thinking needs landmarks. Without landmarks, one cannot think. In the same manner that acting (e.g., moving from one point to another point) needs landmarks and energy to proceed (i.e., acting), thinking is an act that needs landmarks and energy in order to be executed.

Values

Values can be divided into two sub-categories: espoused values and enacted values. Espoused values are those that are explicitly endorsed by the leaders of organizations. On the other hand, enacted values are those that are actually converted into employee behaviors.

Bibliography

Bertalanffy, L. (1968). *General system theory*. New York, NY: George Brazillier.

Darwin, C. (1871). *The descent of man*. London: John Murray.

Einstein, A. (1916, éd. 1956) *La théorie de la relativité restreinte et générale*. Paris: Gauthiers-Villars.

Fearing, F. (1954). An examination of the conceptions of Benjamin Whorf in the light of the theories of perception and cognition. *American Anthropologist*, *54*, 47–81.

Fidaali, K. (1987). *Le Pouvoir du bangré*. Paris: Presse de la Renaissance.
Gibson, J. J. (1979). *The ecological approach to visual perception*. Boston, MA: Houghton Mifflin.
Kahneman, D. (1973). *Attention and effort*. Englewood Cliffs, NJ: Prentice-Hall Inc.
Ocasio, W. (1997). Towards an attention-based view of the firm. *Strategic Management Journal*, *18*(1), 187–206.
Pal, A. R., & Saha, D. (2015). Word sense disambiguation: A survey. *International Journal of Control. Theory and Computer Modeling*, *5*(3), 1–16.
Ravatin, J. (1992). *Théorie des champs de cohérence*. Lyon: Librairie Lacour.
Ravatin, J. (2008). *Développements autour des champs de cohérence. Tome I, 1ère et 2ème partie*. Lyon: Editions du Cosmogone.
Shepherd, D. A., & Sutcliffe, K. M. (2011). Inductive top-down theorizing: A source of new theories of organization. *Academy of Management Review*, *36*(2), 361–380.
Von Wright, G. H. (1968). An essay in deontic logic and the general theory of action. *Acta Philosophica Fennica*, *21*, 1–55.
Wang, S., Liao, J., Xia, D., & Chang, T. (2010). The impact of organizational justice on work performance: Mediating effects of organizational commitment and leader-member exchange. *International Journal of Manpower*, *31*(6), 660–677.
Whorf, B. L. (1956). *Language, thought, and reality*. Cambridge: The MIT Press. Library of Congress Catalog Card Number: 56-5367.

3 Context

In this theoretical essay, the fundamental problem was to examine how and why OJ and MPJ interact, and to what extent such interactions facilitate the management of OC. In order to achieve that goal, one needs to acquire a better understanding of the basic mechanism of social exchanges that produce shared norms (e.g., norms of justice), and to examine to what extent the perceptions of such norms experienced by people at work (e.g., fairness) induce their decision-making (e.g., acceptance, resistance, or neutral), while various levels of change take place over time in organizations. Nevertheless, the issue is not to formulate what is good or bad (e.g., fair or unfair) from an ethical point of view while managing change, but to provide new insights in order to realize successful OC.

Despite the many theories, implementation strategies, and approaches to the management of change, successful OC remains elusive, which explains the poor success rate of program changes in general. Nonetheless, change initiatives are among the most important projects an organization can undertake, as successful outcomes could bring competitive advantages while failure could have catastrophic consequences. While most past studies have defined or examined the consequences of OJ on OC (e.g., willingness or resistance to change), none have considered that most of the time, there is a gap between OJ (i.e., EPJ) and MPJ, which plays a decisive role in the high rate of failure while managing change in organizations. Therefore, this study considered that when it takes place, the management of this gap is a key factor in the success of OC, while introducing a new research question—that is, to what extent can OJ and MPJ be aligned to facilitate change? This gap is particularly important, and it is necessary, through dialog, to build a common understanding between employees and managers in order to explain corporate decisions when radical change takes place (e.g., mergers and acquisitions, corporate restructuring). Thus, as previous studies did not clearly identify this gap and its impact on managing change, there is a need to do so and also to explain why it exists, what its content is (e.g., theoretical components), and how to manage it. Therefore, the research questions that address this issue constitute a novelty within the literature, demonstrating that this research study is original and innovative.

A literature review must be a critical evaluation of materials that have been published more or less in relation to the academic fields of the research topic (e.g., OJ, OC), while considering the progress of research based on a similarity of concepts or theories (e.g., social exchanges or social norms), methodological similarities among the studies reviewed, or historical development of academic fields (e.g., change or justice) that align with the research study. Moreover, since a literature review can be lengthy, it is also essential to divide it into sections and subsections to logically organize the information presented. Therefore, the author identified a set of key meta-words (e.g., perception, change, justice, social exchanges, norms), used as filters for dividing the integrative literature review into three topics. The meta-words are as follows:

- social exchanges, norms, and perceptions of social norms;
- change, perceptions of change, and organizational change;
- justice, norms of justice, and organizational justice.

Thus, applying the inductive top-down theorizing methodology, for each topic the author intertwined personal thoughts (i.e., prior knowledge) with those of other scholars in order to present both his own point of view and those of others who are academically recognized. Such an approach contributes greatly to a critical analysis of the literature.

Literature Review

Social Exchanges and Perceptions of Social Norms vs. Change

Introduced by Homans (1958), social exchanges comprise actions contingent on the rewarding reactions of others, which over time provide for mutually and rewarding transactions and relationships. At various levels of aggregation (i.e., group size), social relations are built with more or less reciprocity and power attached, including more or less trust and negotiation relationships, which determine behaviors and hierarchies of people within groups. Although individuals often fail to recognize socially shared standards, social norms (e.g., folkways, fashions, mores, taboos, laws) are more or less established rules that help to coordinate their interactions (i.e., behaviors) with others. Each rule plays a landmark role for individuals, which helps to build the social game, including norms manipulation.

Originating from social exchanges theory, function, emergence, and maintenance of social norms as conventions are at the heart of most of the social sciences and have received much academic interest. Thus, social norms considered as rules that govern behaviors have been extensively studied by academics, providing three main canonical theories of conformity: socialization, social identity, and rational choice. Nevertheless, due to a lack of evidence explaining how such normative beliefs affect behaviors, all these three theories are deficient because their definitions of what a norm is are too rigid to explain these phenomena.

When socialization is embedded in the concept of a utilitarian framework, while positing that an individual action is equated with a choice among several alternatives, no clear explanation regarding how people take decisions (i.e., selecting one option) is provided. Most of the time, scholars' thoughts become inextricable when they perform multiple experiments without a clear understanding of the phenomenon, particularly when they try to examine the conditions that induce compliance to norms or not. In the same manner, in the theory of social identity, which assumes that norms affect action by becoming part of individual preferences and goals, no clear explanation is provided regarding why people adhere to group behaviors, or how people take decisions to adhere to such groups over time (e.g., managing change), resulting in confusion across discussions that is reinforced due to the introduction of concepts like trust or cooperation, which add no clarity to the debate.

Regarding the rational choice theory, which is related to the belief that norms have to be upheld by sanctions, scholars consider that compliance to norms is a utility maximizing strategy, while using a compliance approach that includes more or less a system of approval/disapproval that doesn't explain how such a system emerges as a meta norm, i.e., a concept that only shifts the problem one level up. However, despite introducing the concept of internalization, which suggests that it is rational to internalize a norm, not all norms involve sanctions. Nevertheless, no one explains why such a process occurs, or how people take such a decision preceding this behavior (i.e., to internalize). Thus, despite many recent attempts to explain social norms, some of which include Bayesian approaches (e.g., evolutionary model), all these theories are more descriptive than explicative, and none provides clear answers regarding the two fundamental questions, which have to do with why norms emerge, and why and how people make the decision to apply them (i.e., to comply). Therefore, by using various approaches such as linguistic analogies or game theories (e.g., evolutionary game), social norms have been progressively modeled to build scales of economic values for assessing social costs.

By contrast, how people perceive such norms in the movement of change (e.g., transformational change) is still not completely understood. Thus, people often perceive and accept a norm simply because they benefit from it (e.g., power or justice). Nevertheless, when someone rejects a widely accepted norm or resists by acting with more or less transgression (i.e., distance), reasons that are often not very well understood (e.g., emotions) are most of the time simply left behind. On this point, scholars know that emotions come up in social exchanges both individually and collectively, and most of them argue that in the workplace the roles of affect (e.g., trust) and fairness operate as landmarks to assess stress versus job satisfaction, while inducing social adaptation initiatives (e.g., education, job design) in order to increase organizational performance.

Thereby, in the absence of consensus, the literature contains different theoretical conceptions of social exchanges (e.g., organizational support theory, psychological contract theory). According to organizational support theory, employees' perceptions of their treatment from their organization are favorable or unfavorable, while most of the time developing an obligation that is either adhesion (i.e., acceptance) or resistance (i.e., dissatisfaction) toward their organizations. In that way, favorable work experiences are perceived and valued to reinforce well-being in the workplace. Such approaches are very one-way utilitarian as people value their work to the extent of what the organization cares about their contribution and well-being.

By contrast, psychological contract theory assumes that both employees and organizations have mutual expectations concerning work conditions and resources to put in, which induces a two-way feedback evaluation promoting reciprocity, which is the heart of any social exchange theory. There is a loop that induces a positive effect because work conditions are positively related to the goals that people have to reach, including their well-being. Then, characteristics of the goals contained in the changes have an impact on work attitudes and positive attitudes toward change (PATC); therefore, non-monetary intrinsic work opportunities have a greater impact on PATC than monetary extrinsic work opportunities, and stress perception (i.e., the perceptions that work demands exceed work resources in the face of professional changes) is negatively related to PATC, while increasing person–organization fit within an organization (i.e., the compatibility between individuals and organizations). Thus, the use of normative behaviors becomes a means of describing organizational culture.

Generally speaking, social norms are the rules and conventions that guide the conduct of members of a society: how we dress, what and how we eat, where and how we travel, our recreation, and the way we work. Social norms, like many other social phenomena, are an unplanned or unexpected result of individuals' interactions, which ought to be understood as a kind of grammar of social interactions. Like a grammar, a system of norms specifies what is acceptable and what is not in a society, and analogously to a grammar, it is not the product of human design. This view suggests that a study of the conditions under which norms come into being, as opposed to one stressing the functions fulfilled by social norms, is important in order to understand the differences between social norms and others types of injunctions, particularly within corporations, such as hypothetical imperatives, moral codes, or legal rules. Therefore, to explain social behavior in terms of norms requires an independent assessment that participants consider the norms to be germane. These authors thus employed a method using part of the work of Fishbein (1967) and those of Schwartz and Tessler (1972), while trying to assess normative beliefs in predicting behavior intentions.

Otherwise, when discussing from a methodological point of view, persons prefer to state that norms reflect their personal sense of what is right and proper rather than compare them from the examples and expectations of others. Hence, it seems that the best way to determine whether a norm can be applied is to compare the personal response to the norm with the feelings perceived at the moment of the response. The latter would be expected if the behavior has occurred and if it was considered as normative.

Nevertheless, some norms or conventions become more rigid, and then progressively transform into more or less explicit rules, which are different from norms because a rule requires or prohibits behaviors (e.g., being a student means following some rules). Moreover, most of the time, there are sanctions attached to rules if they are not applied. This means that rules are often set up by a body (e.g., individuals or organizations like states) having authority over those who have to follow the rules that have been set.

By contrast, norms are often considered as conventions that emerge from habits or behaviors coming from the bottom of the field, while most of the time rules are the result of a top-down process. Nevertheless, there are organizations (e.g., Japanese organizations) that are more or less managed from the bottom up. These varied management structures lead to actors playing various political roles, which are factors of resistance or willingness vis-à-vis change. Then, people's behaviors inside organizations become more politically oriented, and the perceptions of change and the perceptions of justice become more intertwined, particularly when organizational politics (OP) occur. Therefore, perceptions of OP are very important aspects of organizational life with respect to its members as these influence various processes, which ultimately affect the performance of employees.

Further, using various attitudes and behaviors, such studies investigate the relationship of perceptions of OP with the multidimensional performance of employees, which is measured individually (e.g., organizational citizenship behavior) or collectively (i.e., organizational) for assessing employees' performance simultaneously. Thus, the process through which these perceptions operate is also investigated by these authors in the light of social exchange theory and reciprocity norms. Most of the time, OP perceptions in workplaces are viewed as empirical evidence of its negative relationship with job satisfaction, organizational commitment, and job performance, while Folger, Konovsky, and Cropanzano (1992) concluded that these negative perceptions about OP make employees feel as if they are working in an unjust and unfair environment, which makes them dissatisfied and as a result they are compelled to quit from the department or organization.

Employee behavior at work is very important to understand, as this affects performance and productivity, while reciprocity norms and social exchanges become important outcomes of employee interactions that flourish within organizations, and expectations of reward motivate or demotivate the workers. Nevertheless, employees at work need to be managed. Therefore, relationships between OJ (i.e., the process) and MPJ (i.e., perception of justice of who performs the process) need to be examined without forgetting the role of board values facing the pressure of institutional logics (e.g., public interest groups, governmental regulators, and institutional investors), which are more or less embedded into both agency theory and socio-political perspectives.

From the author's perspective, organization and social exchanges start with two people (i.e., more than one), and expand progressively according to boundaries decided most of the time by these first promoters. Then, a third person comes along, and triadic substitutes to dyadic relationships open up new opportunities (e.g., behavioral game) for the nascent group forming the root of social capital (i.e., shared norms). Therefore, the author believes that before examining social exchanges within the literature, two key antecedents need to be highlighted, which shape behavioral games and allow social exchanges. These antecedents include the role of attention in the process of perception, and the role of communication in organizations, which are more or less conducted according to self-interest during the process of perception of justice.

Regarding the role of attention in the process of perception, it can be associated with the internal mechanism that determines the significance of stimuli (i.e., data coming from sense), and thereby makes it impossible to predict behavior by stimulus consideration alone. Attention is controllable (meaning that the organism appears to control the choice of stimuli that will be allowed, in turn, to control its behavior) and selective (i.e., the organism selectively attends to some stimuli, or aspects of stimulation, in preference to others), which are functions that require an effort. When people perceive, their attention must first be mobilized. In other terms, it is hard to conceive perception without attention, and people often do not perceive something only because their attention has not been mobilized. Moreover, some sensory representations occur as results of the mechanism that operates emotional intelligence, while conceptual representations are progressively forming as a result of the mechanism that operates verbal intelligence, as some authors have already highlighted when theorizing.

Regarding the role of communication in organizations, in everyday life, building ways of communication is an obligation as soon as we are not alone. That is why language exists as a foundation of verbal intelligence. Without words or signs, it is difficult to communicate. Therefore, languages across human beings are more or less rich in symbols (e.g., words and signs) with a variety of meanings (i.e., interpretations). All often vary (i.e., change) according to environmental characteristics that we have invented as landmarks (e.g., scale, location, time), while increasing the precision and complexity of our thoughts (i.e., human knowledge). In the same way that attention is not always mobilized, people often do not communicate even when they perceive something. Nevertheless, communication is a voluntary act (i.e., decision to communicate), which is not necessarily the case when attention is mobilized (e.g., reflex action).

Change, Perception of Change, and Organizational Change

Many (perhaps most) research questions in management implicitly—even if not framed as such—address issues of change. A lot of academic works have more or less mentioned or invoked the role of contexts, while change takes place without a clear definition of what a context is and how human beings interact with its complexity. Highlighted by Kirk (1954), Heraclitus already thought that there is nothing permanent except change, and an understanding of human systems of thinking has turned out to be fundamental to any study of change. Scholars know that environmental factors (e.g., contexts) contribute substantially to the development of intelligence, but they do not yet clearly understand what those factors are or how they work (Neisser et al., 1996). Thus, considering intelligence more as a process, there is a need to set up a theoretical framework that helps to get a better understanding of how contexts and behaviors interact dynamically, while occurring change and risks.

Therefore, in the field of organizational behavior, Johns (2006) argued in his introduction that the impact of context on organizational behavior is not sufficiently recognized or appreciated by researchers. Then, after an attempt to define contexts and its dimensions, he concluded: "What has been lacking, I submit, is comparable progress in understanding how context affects organizational behavior" (p. 404). Such a comment proves that at the level of an organization, there is still a need to get a better understanding of how people make a myriad of decisions (e.g., interpretations of perceptions) over time in context (e.g., corporate finance), while emotions play a central role for regulation in the workplace.

Thus, the author believes that no human system of thinking, which is based on interpretation of perceptions, can be considered as complete without providing a few theoretical foundations on how behaviors and contexts interact, while norms emerge and disappear amongst an infinity of landmarks (e.g., social norms through social exchanges). Consequently, there is a need to respond to why and how contexts and behaviors interact, and more precisely according to the particular environments of organizational behavior: how to balance behaviors and contexts in order to reinforce techniques of decision-making (e.g., judgment of fairness) on a daily and normal basis, and particularly when people are facing an unknown (e.g., uncertainty of forecasts) with risk of relative deprivation or disruptive environments (e.g., strategic or radical change in organizations) due to marketing strategy.

Although change is a process of continual renewal, in order to facilitate the categorization of perceptions of change, many scholars suggest defining change using the categories by the rate of occurrence, by how it comes about, and by scale, while some others scholars like Kezar (2001) stated that "organizational change varies by what model the reader uses to examine it" (p. 12).

Her work suggests a common language for understanding organizational change and provides a classification based on:

- Degree of change
- Timing of change
- Scale of change
- Focus of change
- Adaptive/generative
- Intentionality: planned versus unplanned change
- Target of change: change process and outcomes.

Degree of change is differentiated between first-order and second-order change. A first-order change is a minor adjustment and improvement in one or a few dimensions of the organization; it does not change the organization's core. A second-order change is transformational change seeking to alter values or mission, culture, functioning processes, and structure of the organization.

Nevertheless, defining change alone does not appear to be helpful for managing change, nor for balancing effects or for cracking its code, and such descriptive categories do not help to explain how human beings perceive change and how they decide about change over time.

Therefore, due to the rate of failure in implementing changes—70%—one can say there is a basic lack of a valid framework of how to successfully implement and manage OC, whether for changing routines, navigating paradox, or for managing innovation and strategic change, or radical change. However, today, two conceptions of perceiving change and managing OC currently coexist in the literature (i.e., planned and emergent).

First, Kurt Lewin's (1951) *planned* approach with his three-step model (i.e., unfreezing, moving, and refreezing) has dominated the field during the last few decades. Viewing the organization as a mechanical system, which needs leadership to proceed, this approach has been promoted by various authors, while providing a set of theoretical and practical contributions (e.g., field theory, group dynamics, action research). Nevertheless, criticism appeared, and new issues have been introduced like the role of conversation or institutionalization, while other studies have pointed out weaknesses (e.g., appropriateness and efficacy), all leading to a call for an alternative, which is suggested by the *emergent* approach.

Second, due to a more complex and evolving business environment (e.g., globalization, multiculturalism), considering organizations as living systems, the emergent approach of change is considered by some authors as universal. Nevertheless, mainly because an organization as an *open system* needs to interact permanently with its environment, which is unique at a given time, a rule that succeeds in one organization fails in another. Thus, organizations need to adapt over time to turbulent contexts by choosing the right position for decision-making (e.g., bottom-up versus top-down) at the right time. Thereby, recognizing the complexity of contexts, the emergent approach promotes agility (i.e., ability to move and to make sense facing change), providing more autonomy to employees for reacting, while managing the complexity of change (e.g., contingencies, breakdowns, and opportunities).

Nevertheless, whatever the varying definitions of an organization (e.g., open system or social construct), and despite the fact that change can be viewed differently (e.g., discrete event or continuous process) using various theoretical approaches like complex adaptive system and models (e.g., Burke & Litwin's model (1992), Kotter's eight-step model (2007)), there is consensus on the fact that OC must be approached from a multidisciplinary perspective. Few authors advocate that OC theories are not useful.

On the contrary, most scholars argue that one can benefit from various theoretical perspectives on OC, while others who are guided by strict observance of behavioral theories highlight the mechanical role of rules (e.g., norms) and process (e.g., discourse), which operationalize organizations. Moreover, in today's workplace, the fact that most managers spend their lifetime within different cultures, leads to consideration of the role of cross-cultural management in OC processes. Nevertheless, questions remain: How can organizations manage change when they operate inside boundaries while change has no border? How can one delimit organizational boundaries, and manage at the frontiers, norms and change that take place on both sides? All of this questioning is more about what to trust means while social exchanges occur at the frontiers, which is an issue related to the social capital grid and to norms of citizenship.

Mixing bonding/bridging social capital seems to be a solution advocated by some scholars. Furthermore, to what extent does such a balance occur when people need to use norms for assessing their perceptions? People in the workplace (i.e., inside) are coming from outside where they are spending most of their life within different cultures, which leads to putting more emphasis on the importance of the role of individual social norms more or less shared in OC (e.g., habits, folkways, mores, taboo).

When scholars respond to the question "Who says change can be managed?", these authors argue that the answer to this question depends upon the underlying image one has of both managing and change. *Managing* means the ways of thinking and how to act (i.e., behaviors), while change is related to how to deal with the continuous variations of the environment (i.e., contexts). Therefore, by using various lenses of academic disciplines, many scholars have tried to get a better understanding of how contexts and behaviors interact. Without entering into the discussion of how to define human rationality (i.e., human intelligence), and the well-known definition given by Darwin (1871) as the ability to adapt behaviors facing environments, without forgetting the added value carried by the relativity of behaviors promoted by Einstein (1916), no attempt has yet succeeded in establishing a *continuum* capable of explaining how behaviors and contexts interact with the aim to better manage their interactions.

Thus, various schools of thinking split the issue across different approaches. The behaviorist approach is deterministic: people's behavior is assumed to be entirely controlled by their environment and their prior learning, so they do not play any part in choosing their own actions. Modern behavior analysis has also witnessed a massive resurgence in research and applications related to language and cognition, with the development of relational frame theory. In the second half of the 20th century, behaviorism was largely eclipsed as a result of the cognitive revolution. More recently, studies have been done on physical intelligence with the aim to extend the concept of affordance, using linear or non-linear causalities while introducing a new paradigm where the brain is not considered as the seat of intelligence.

Nevertheless, none of these schools of thinking have succeeded in modeling the function "understand", or to establish a consistent, general, and useful theory for responding to the questions of why and how behaviors and contexts interact, and how human beings are making decisions over time based on such interactions. Thus, instead of bringing clarity to this issue, most past studies around these research questions have brought confusion, and some have added complexity—for example, Sotolongo (2002) asked at the beginning of his article: "From where does social complexity emerge?" (p. 105). Then, trying to understand what changes in social change, despite the use of the concept of affordance described hereafter, he did not succeed in clarifying the relations among changes, behaviors and contexts, arguing that complexity generates affordance, while posing the question of boundaries.

The affordances of the environment are what it offers the animal, what it provides or furnishes, either for good or ill. An affordance is a resource that the environment offers any animal that has the capabilities to perceive and use it. When used in this sense, the term affordance refers to the perceived and actual properties of the thing, primarily those fundamental properties that determine just how the thing could be used. A chair affords ("is for") support, and, therefore, affords to sit. From the author's perspective, affordance theory has not yet been understood deeply nor used enough. Moreover, when properly combined with deontic logic, affordance theory should allow increasing knowledge about how people make decisions over time, whatever contexts they are in (e.g., verbal disambiguation). Thus, some attempts have recently been made using adaptive deontic logic to set up normative conflicts for discussing situations in which an agent ought to do each of a number of things but cannot do them all. Sadly, Goble (2013) concluded that his adaptive deontic logic is not the way to address the problem posed by normative conflicts, while suggesting the need to find a deontic logic that really does accommodate these normative conflicts.

Other researchers are more focused on moral issues. Assuming that people are motivated by a sense of duty, obligation, and moral virtue, some scholars consider *deontic justice* as the phenomenon of justice for justice's sake, while others claim the notion of *deonance* based on Kantian ethics with the idea that people's cognitive processes and behaviors are compelled by *categorical imperative*, or *a priori* universal ethical principles of an innate and/or selfless nature. Nevertheless, such moral-oriented research is unable to explain the decision-making process involved in producing *normal* or *deviant* behaviors (e.g., moral outrage). Thus, due to the variety of cultural appraisals of what is good or not, more or less built into social exchanges (e.g., trust), which inevitably occur over time in multi-agent systems, instead of increasing complexity of the analysis with *a priori* (e.g., comparative goodness or betterness), or consideration of moral prejudice, there is a need to get a better understanding of how human rationality works for decision-making in the face of a diversity of contexts, with no obligation to call for a punishment system (e.g., retributive justice), with more or less self-regulation, which most of the time does not allow the use of all potential that deontic logic offers. Nevertheless, none of the above research orientations are able to provide theoretical proposals with enough clarity and simplicity (i.e., compatible with what happens in real time in real life) to explain human behaviors. Such a lack probably explains why until today, change has not yet been simply defined to account for its duality, because nobody has yet clearly linked its double components, which are respectively, the environment of the observer and the observer itself—but, to achieve that goal, as previously mentioned, one must be able to construct a *continuum* between contexts and human behaviors.

From the author's perspective, change (i.e., variation) is a continuous process. There are two categories of change, which explain that the word *complexity* is most often associated with this concept. One is a change that happens in context. This change is a non-stop process because the environment always varies. The other is because the observer that I am changes itself over time (i.e., behavior). Both constitute probably a continuum that needs to be addressed in practice with the aim to separate contextual constituents of the environment (i.e., desegmentation), and—in theory—for providing rules that allow managing the results of such desegmentation (i.e., a theoretical proposal). Moreover, each change is also a risk. Then, we have two categories of risks (i.e., risks of contexts) due to variation of contexts, and risk of behaviors due to variation of behaviors. This double process defines a systemic. Therefore, each decision for change has the risk of increasing more or less resistance, while inducing behaviors, which depends of contexts, and all these relations increase complexity due to a loop effect producing change and risks attached. Thus, these double change components (i.e., change of context and change of behavior) intertwine over time, providing infinite variations of realities (i.e., perceptions of the environment) within the many ambiguities that need to be managed (i.e., complexity). Although it is impossible to account for all the realities of such complexity, it is possible to conceive why and how they are produced and why and how humans select some of them (i.e., disambiguation mechanism), and then look at what they do with them. Then, such an approach helps to better understand (i.e., to construct shared meanings) why and how people behave (i.e., causality behavior), and particularly what are the reasons for (e.g., interest)—i.e., why—and what are the ways of (e.g., intention, volition)—i.e., how—one person behaves with another (i.e., managing *attention* using communication means) in order to achieve various goals of doing something or not with others (e.g., playing, working, fighting, etc.), which is sometimes done just for enhancing, one more time, the self-experimentation of PCM.

While most human experiences (e.g., verbal or emotional) are reinforcing the principle of hierarchies and some others the basic principles of group living (e.g., motivation for and benefit of), copying from naturalistic observations, some human constructs (e.g., organizations) help to navigate planned or unplanned asymmetries of change (i.e., living with the uncertainty of everyday life).

Regarding OC, one first has to examine how the observer detects change. Change detection has been mainly studied through the lens of visual perception while distinguishing between motion and difference. In his research, Rensink (2000, 2002) denoted not only detection proper (i.e., the change report of the observer), but also the identification of change (i.e., what change is) with the addition of localization, which in my opinion is a part of the identification. Furthermore, visual perceptions are closely related to verbal expressions (e.g., one learns to read while pointing to a part of the environment with the index finger). Then, the process of managing visual change perceptions is related to the process of managing meanings (i.e., verbal disambiguation) that each of us activates when a decision is made to deal with this change detection, and despite an infinite set of environments and diversity of human beings, this underlying process (i.e., the skeleton) is always the same. Therefore, during such a process, the intention of the observer is a contingency, which does not modify the process itself, and, consequently, it is not an antecedent of perception like attention, but most of the time already a consequence of a decision that has been made by the observer. Thus, without entering deeply into the bio-physical interpretation of the visual mechanism, however, the manner of change detection is defined, the conscious detection of change cannot be separated from the process of human understanding itself and the manner with which human beings manage their own interpretations, which is the final process that must be investigated.

From the author's perspective, understanding the disambiguation process is a *golden key* to any theory of understanding (e.g., artificial intelligence), and particularly when people want to design smart computers due to the central place of verbal understanding (i.e., meanings management of words) that verbal intelligence produces. Thus, providing new insights into the way we experience the world around us is important, but it is not enough. Consequently, *understanding of understanding* is still an open *grand challenge*, and a small step ahead in this grand challenge is a large step ahead for the whole of humanity.

Otherwise, one cannot examine OC without providing a definition of what organization is, or responding to the following question: What does it mean to organize? In everyday life, building communication means is a must as soon as we are not alone. That is why language exists. Languages across human beings are more or less rich in symbols (e.g., words and signs) with a variety of meanings (i.e., interpretations). All often vary (i.e., change) according to environmental characteristics that we have invented as landmarks (e.g., scale, location, time), while increasing the precision and complexity of our thoughts (i.e., human knowledge). When two persons meet, a process begins. Each is going to progressively discover what to do or not do with the other. According to their differences or resemblances, such a process is a multiform process using the communication means of each person, in order to build with the other what people call a relation. In fact, multiple relations are simultaneously undertaken, and some connections that are made are more useful to bridge and then reinforce what they are or are not doing together.

These relationships are the basic unit of analysis for any organizational perspective, because they are the roots of a social construct (i.e., more than one), called social capital, which is more or less defined by shared norms. Thus, defining organization is a matter of boundaries (i.e., who is included) and contents (i.e., for what purpose), independently of the rules of governance that are applied (e.g., democratic vs. authoritarian). Then, once one has gained a good understanding of the challenges to managing change, it becomes easier to examine what are the better conditions to organize readiness for change in organizations, particularly with the aim of reducing resistance to these changes.

The choices that people make when they assess justice in the workplace can be assimilated as a choice of value. Such values can be divided into two sub-categories: espoused values and enacted values. Espoused values are those that are explicitly endorsed by the leaders of organizations. On the other hand, enacted values are those that are actually converted into employee behaviors. According to Ostroff et al. (2003), the difference between espoused and enacted values is important because the gap is related to employees' attitudes and behaviors (p. 568). Such concepts of value highlight the potential gap mentioned by the author while questioning again the role of context that can be more or less favorable to change (i.e., readiness vs. resistance).

Individual readiness for change is a key to successful change, while commitment is a psychological mechanism that helps organizational processes (e.g., change) to be implemented. Three types of commitment (i.e., affective, continuance, and normative) are considered by scholars to have an impact in the workplace. While both affective and normative bring emotional attachment respectively to the task (i.e., job design) and to the organization, continuance is related to earnings. The last has the lowest ability to guide behaviors, while affective and continuance represent underlying motives of loyalty with more or less resistance to change embedded.

Resistance to change describes an approach toward change as one not readily embracing it by those it affects, taking into account the cognitive, behavioral, and affective elements, rendering it a three-dimensional construct. Silence, fear, opposition, or disinterest are often early signals to resistance. While an "open system" highlights the systemic nature of change, "social construct" tries to make sense of it. Nevertheless, in both cases, resistance to change alters when it does not prevent the transformation of organizations. Whatever the variables used to characterize change, according to Connor (1995) there are common factors that impact resistance to change, including:

- Lack of trust
- Belief that change is unnecessary

- Belief that change is not feasible
- Economic threats
- Relative high cost
- Fear of personal failure
- Loss of status and power
- Threat to values and ideals
- Resentment of interference

Moreover, the forces that exert pressures for making changes (e.g., technical, political, and cultural) increase the complexity of leading change and inertia due to imprinting. While Scott et al. (2014) recently examined whether managers act fairly, Peus, Frey, Gerkhardt, Fischer, and Traut-Mattausch (2008) pointed out the need to examine the negative relationship generally found between OC and employee attitudes (e.g., counterproductive work behaviors, absenteeism, withdrawal), which are often the result of emotional exhaustion (e.g., burnout) that influences perceptions of justice and resistance to change. Thus, the dynamic of the gap between EPJ and MPJ plays a role similar to that of emotional factors for aligning sense-making and reducing negative response to change, particularly when people need to assess the legitimacy of their fellow humans.

Justice, Norms of Justice, and Organizational Justice

Justice

Most of the time, scholars consider that justice and social exchanges are interweaved in the workplace. Nevertheless, despite many research studies based on organizational support like reciprocity, how people perceive justice is a problematic issue not yet completely resolved. Festinger (1957) argued that when people are uncertain about their opinions or abilities, they evaluate themselves by comparing themselves to others who are similar. Adams (1963) advocated that people pursue a balance between the investments (e.g., time, attention, commitment) and the rewards (e.g., status, gratitude, pay) gained from these relationships. Moreover, both internal factors (e.g., level of participation in decision-making, role of ambiguity, or role of conflict) and external factors influence perceptions of justice (e.g., culture). Consequently, such impacts on perceptions of justice, which sometimes are able to corrupt the consistency principle of OJ itself (e.g., terrorism), must all be taken into account when people assess the effects of subjectivity or objectivity on perceptions of justice by the systems of control. Whatever the timing, negative outcomes (e.g., social deprivation) occur when people receive less than what they are entitled to receive in comparison to others.

Inequality aversion as an outcome of social deprivation leads to a lot of studies that account for strong disapproval of unequal treatments, particularly when equality rules are highly institutionalized in context; this posits the question of the costs of norms enforcement and punishments in cases of deviant behavior. Thus, inequality and inequity are considered the two main negative externalities of social norm's theory, which induce more or less norm's infringement. Beyond justice theory (Rawls, 1971; Sen, 2012), applied at work, most researchers have examined the linear effects of inequity; few have looked at the consequences of feeling better off than others, even fewer have assessed the circumstances when the intra-personal versus the interpersonal applies, and none have clearly pointed out that the concept of equality itself should be reexamined.

This lack of judgment is strange. Probably because most people are convinced that the equality concept is a reality, while it is only an artifact that has been invented a long time ago for geometric purposes first (i.e., comparison) and then widely used for calculus. Most people are not even aware of their need to conform. They live under the illusion that they follow their own ideas and inclinations, that they are individuals, that they have arrived at their opinions as a result of their own thinking, and that it just happens that their ideas are the same as those of the majority. At the same time, most people fear their differences while claiming the right to be different.

Norms of Justice

While some authors have attempted to model the interactions between norms or justice and perceptions of justice, highlighting concepts like sense-giving or sense-making, others have included a more contextual approach like downsizing. In most of these studies, equality, need, and equity are the norms of justice, which play a central role with trust for OJ, and particularly for interpersonal trust within negotiations (e.g., for achieving cooperative strategy, while players allocate scare resources). Although there is a consensus among scholars regarding the role of perceptions of justice in the management of change, a fundamental question remains about the high rate of failure of OC. Compared to the large number and origin diversity of theoretical studies on justice, whatever the approach of OJ more or less related to OC, including normative or descriptive approaches or spatial environment, very few scholars have recently examined critically, as Singer did (2015), whether change failures in justice (e.g., social injustice) result from faulty norms of justice, which are currently based on the principle of equality (e.g., reciprocity) and embedded into a rational choice without explaining how such a choice is made.

Certainly, when people claim that men are created equal—as Sen had noticed—such claim serves largely to deflect attention from the fact that we are physically and socially different. Nevertheless, despite good intentions, which for the Kantians is theoretically enough, in practice, such a philosophical approach doesn't provide any tool for solving how to manage change on a daily basis, while enhancing justice across people. Therefore, one needs to practice *integrative thinking*, while using radical assumption (e.g., new paradigm) for transforming into reality such a reasoning that is so embedded in the egalitarian paradigm, in which equality is a reality (i.e., a mean) and most often the ultimate objective (i.e., end).

From the author's perspective, equality (i.e., =) is only a convention that became a habit of human beings, mainly because it allows their rationality to categorize. Then, progressively, that convention became a belief, useful but always false in real life, which introduces a *bias* in current norms of justice that most of the time is based on the concept of *reciprocity,* itself a social expression of equality with fairness attached. Such above individual *selbstverblendung* explains why some challenges are so difficult to overcome—like managing change, justice, or big data (i.e., data that human beings cannot easily categorize)—and why such challenges are associated with complexity.

Recently, considering that it is crucial for developing theories allowing organizations to get practical outcomes during periods of change, research calls for a more dynamic conceptualization of OJ in the workplace, and a better understanding of perceptions of justice, Organizational scholars contend that employees will assume a positive approach to OC if they perceive their treatment by management and the organization as being fair.

Most scholars argue that employees' perceptions of trust and fairness impact the success of the change initiative, while others advocate that OJ is key to succeeding in any OC. Whatever arguments push forward, there is a need to clearly understand what "being fair" means and what are the norms of justice that people are using to assess such justice with trust or distrust, through their own perceptions of justice.

Moreover, two important points need to be carefully taken into account to tackle such kind of research.

- First, when research is based on interpretation of perceptions, the context in which interpretations are made of these perceptions is key to understanding the meaning expressed verbally (i.e., consciously) by the person performing such acts (i.e., perceiving and interpreting).
- Second, due to the unique rationality of each subject matter expert (e.g., scholars) and the dynamic nature of the environments in which they proceed, there is a need to set up a theoretical framework able to account for how behaviors and contexts interact dynamically (i.e., change), with the aim of reducing the complexity of these interactions in order to become manageable.

Furthermore, we know that OJ depends on norms of justice, their interpretations, and the willingness to act according to rules that these norms suggest to people within contexts that change over time. In addition, regarding the dynamics and complexity of social exchanges, some authors have stated that economics and management theories could profit from a clearer understanding of shared norms. Therefore, one needs a deeper understanding of why and how perceptions of justice interact (i.e., OJ and MPJ) during a change in organizations.

OJ describes the views of employees on the fairness of treatment within an organization, while organizational trust refers to faith in the system, culture, and structure of the organization in which an employee works.

Organizational Justice

Organizational justice describes the views of employees on the fairness of treatment within an organization, which is commonly separated into three distinctive components: distributive, procedural, and interactional.

Distributive Justice

On the basis of ethical and objective factors, this term describes the same treatment given to similar employees and different treatments for different employees. Distributive justice is conceptualized as the fairness associated with decision outcomes and distribution of tangible (e.g., pay) or intangible resources (e.g., praise), while such fairness increases when outcomes are perceived as being equally applied.

Procedural Justice

Procedural justice is a term used to refer to the views of employees on the justness employed in the means and procedures used to control or manage a process. Procedural justice is defined as the fairness associated with the processes that lead to outcomes and distribution of tangible resources. More people have a voice to become involved, and more justice is perceived.

Interactional Justice

Interactional justice focuses on the way people are treated. More explanations with respect are provided, and more justice is perceived. Colquitt (2001) divides this concept into two components: interpersonal justice, which reflects the thought given to the situations of people, and the civility and compassion exhibited for a person's feelings, with focus on respect and on how to deliver information, while informational justice, which refers to the justness as viewed by the employees of the information utilized in making a decision focuses on the why, timeliness, and truthfulness of the information delivered.

Other scholars advocate for a multi-foci justice approach providing multiple outcomes of OC.

Overview

Articles and books that have significant outcomes are summarized in Table 3.1.

The following criteria were used to make such a selection:

- Seminal work on which theoretical proposals are related
- Direct contribution to open-mindedness of the author
- Clarity of content that increases understanding of the phenomena

Although the selection is coherent with chosen criteria, preconceived notions (e.g., a theorist's idiosyncratic knowledge of the literature) about what is important directed and focused the attention of the author. Thus, a lot of biases have been developed as a consequence of theorists' own interests and prior knowledge.

Amongst scholars, there is more or less a consensus of reasoning within the egalitarian paradigm, in which equality of treatment is key to promoting equality, trust, and fairness, while norms of justice (e.g., fairness) are most of the time based on reciprocity (i.e., social expression of equality). Nevertheless, interactions between OJ and MPJ have not yet been precisely examined, mainly because there is a lack of clear understanding of how contexts and behaviors interact dynamically.

Furthermore, some observations can be made as follows:

- Understanding change is to understand the way we experience the world around us.
- There is a structural gap between any human perceptions (e.g., change or justice), just because of their uniqueness and the uniqueness of the context in which they exist.
- Current norms of justice are mainly based on the principle of reciprocity, which is the social expression of a human artifact (i.e., a social belief) named *equality*. Moreover, a hypothesis of faulty norms of justice is open, particularly when such norms are used for corporate governance. Therefore, the political consequences (i.e., ends, ways, and means to organize human beings) of the above artifact (i.e., =), which is always false in real life, must be examined thoroughly.

Table 3.1 An overview of significant topics and sources of data

Topic	*Study*	*Principle finding(s)/Conclusion(s)*
Attention	Kahneman (1973)	Attention is limited, but the limit is variable from moment to moment. Attention is dividable and allocation of attention is a matter of degree. Attention is selective and controllable to facilitate the processing of selecting perceptual units.
	Occasio (1997)	Attention of decision-maker shapes organization of the firm, which influences the selection of the content of attentional complexes.
Change detection	Rensink (2002)	Attentional management involves the high-level knowledge of the observer.
Field of coherence	Rensink (2000)	Two successive structures are temporally coherent, if they refer to the same object, extended over time.
	Ravatin (2008)	The human being, when he thinks, is related to a field of coherence. Humans were put in a cage where they frolic, but most of them do not know of the existence of this cage.
Relativity of categories	Fearing (1954)	The different language systems lead to fundamental different world-views.
	Whorf (1956)	The languages of living beings themselves determine what each individual who practices them, perceives of the world and thinks.
	Fidaali (1987)	No human thinking is possible without arbitrary conventions.
Systemic	Bertallanfy (1968)	Unlike animals, man himself creates the world, which we call human culture.
Affordances	Gibson (1979)	The medium, substances, surfaces, objects, places, and other animals have affordances for a given animal. They offer benefit or injury, life or death. This is why they need to be perceived.
Theory of action	Von Mises (1949)	Human activity is one arrangement by which the change occurs.
Context	Johns (2006)	Context is a shaper of meaning. Context is a configuration or bundle of stimuli.
Deontic logic	Von Wright (1951)	Deontic propositions are sometimes, or perhaps always, relative to some so-called moral code. What is obligatory within one moral code may be forbidden within another.
Ternary logic	Arpasi (2003)	A brief introduction to ternary logic.
Rationality unknowns	Neisser, et al. (1996)	Every individual has a biological as well as a social environment one that begins in the womb and extends throughout life.
Equality vs. Inequality	Sen (1992)	Deep analysis of equality and inequality into egalitarian paradigm.
Rawl's contestation	Singer (2015)	John Rawls' theory of justice cannot be applied effectively to questions of business ethics and corporate governance.
Distributive justice	Wang, et al. (2010)	Promoting the same treatment of similar employees and different treatment of different employees.

Bibliography

Adams, J. S. (1963). Towards an understanding of inequity. *Journal of Abnormal and Social Psychology*, *67*(5), 422–436.

Arpasi, J. P. (2003). A brief introduction to ternary logic. Retrieved from http://aymara.org/ternary/ternary.pdf. (Accessed 2020).

Bertalanffy, L. (1968). *General system theory*. New York: George Brazillier.

Burke, W. W., & Litwin, G. H. (1992). A causal model of organizational performance and change. *Journal of Management*, *8*(3), 523–546.

Colquitt, J. A. (2001). On the dimensionality of organizational justice: A construct validation of a measure. *Journal of Applied Psychology*, *86*(3), 356–400.

Connor, D. R. (1995). *Managing at the speed of change: How resilient managers succeed and prosper where others fail*. New York: Villard Books.

Darwin, C. (1871). *The descent of man*. London: John Murray.

Einstein, A. (1916, éd. 1956). *La théorie de la relativité restreinte et générale*. Paris: Gauthiers-Villars.

Fearing, F. (1954). An examination of the conceptions of Benjamin Whorf in the light of the theories of perception and cognition. *American Anthropologist*, *54*, 47–81.

Festinger, L. (1957). *Theory of cognitive dissonance*. Evanston, IL: Row Peterson.

Fidaali, K. (1987). *Le Pouvoir du bangré*. Paris: Presse de la Renaissance.

Fishbein, M. (1967). Attitude and the prediction of behavior. In M. Fishbein (Ed.), *Readings in attitude theory and measurement* (pp. 477–492). New York, NY: Wiley.

Folger, R., Konovsky, M. A., & Cropanzano, R. (1992). A due process metaphor for performance appraisal. *Research in Organizational Behavior*, *14*, 129–177.

Gibson, J. J. (1979). *The ecological approach to visual perception*. Boston, MA: Houghton Mifflin.

Goble, L. (2013). Deontic logic (adapted) for normative conflicts. *Logic Journal of the IGPL*, *22*(2), 206–235.

Homans, G. C. (1958). Social behavior as exchange. *American Journal of Sociology*, *63*(6), 597–606.

Johns, G. (2006). The essential impact of context on organizational behavior. *Academy of Management Review*, *31*(2), 386–408.

Kahneman, D. (1973). *Attention and effort*. Englewood Cliffs, NJ: Prentice-Hall Inc.

Kezar, A. J. (2001). Understanding and facilitating organizational change in the 21st century: Recent research and conceptualizations. *ASHE–ERIC Higher Education Report*, *28*(4). San Francisco, CA: Jossey-Bass.

Kirk, G. S. (1954). *Heraclitus. The cosmic fragments*. Cambridge: University Press.

Kotter, J. P. (2007). Leading change. Why transformation efforts fail. *Harvard Business Review*, January 2007, 96–103.

Lewin, K. (1951). *Field theory in social science*. New York: Harper.

Neisser, U., Boodoo, G., Bouchard, T. J., Boykin, A. W., Brody, N., Ceci, S. J., & Urbina, S. (1996). Intelligence: Knowns and unknowns. *The American Psychological Association, Inc.*, *51*(2), 77–101.

Ocasio, W. (1997). Towards an attention-based view of the firm. *Strategic Management Journal*, *18*(1), 187–206.

Ostroff, C., Kinicki, A. J., & Tamkins, M. M. (2003). Organizational culture and climate. In W. C. Borman, D. R. Ilgen, & R. J. Klimoski (Eds.), *Handbook of psychology. Industrial and organizational psychology* (pp. 565–593). Hoboken, NJ: Wiley.

Peus, C., Frey, D., Gerkhardt, M., Fischer, P., & Traut-Mattausch, E. (2008). Leading and managing organizational change initiatives. *Management Revue, 20*(2), 158–175.

Ravatin, J. (2008). *Développements autour des champs de cohérence*. Tome I, 1ère et 2ème partie. Lyon: Editions du Cosmogone.

Rawls, J. (1971). *A theory of justice*. Cambridge, MA: Harvard University Press.

Rensink, R. A. (2000). The dynamic representation of scenes. *Visual Cognition, 7*(1–3), 17–42.

Rensink, R. A. (2002). Change detection. *Annual Review of Psychology, 53*, 245–277.

Schwartz, S. H., & Tessler, R. C. (1972). A test of a model for reducing attitude–behavior discrepancies. *Journal of Personality and Social Psychology, 24*, 224–236.

Scott, B. A., Garza, A. S., Conlon, D. E., & Kim, Y. J. (2014). Why do managers act fairly in the first place? A daily investigation of "Hot" and "Cold" motives and discretion. *Academy of Management Journal, 57*(6), 1571–1591.

Sen, A. K. (1992). *Inequality reexamined*. Cambridge, MA: Harvard University Press.

Sen, A. K. (2012). *L'idée de justice*. Champs: Flammarion.

Singer, A. (2015). There is no Rawlsian theory of corporate governance. *Business Ethics Quarterly, 25*(1), 65–92.

Sotolongo, P. (2002). Complexity, society and everyday life. *Emergence: Complexity and Organization, 4*(1), 105–116.

Von Mises, L. (1949, ed. 1985). *L'action humaine: Traité d'économie*. Paris: P.U.F.

Von Wright, G. H. (1951, ed. 2007). Deontic logic. *Mind, New Series, 60*(237), 1–15.

Wang, S., Liao, J., Xia, D., & Chang, T. (2010). The impact of organizational justice on work performance: Mediating effects of organizational commitment and leader-member exchange. *International Journal of Manpower, 31*(6), 660–677.

Whorf, B. L. (1956). *Language, thought, and reality*. Cambridge: MIT Press. Library of Congress Catalog Card Number: 56–5367.

Part II

Methodology, Findings and Outcomes

4 Methodology

The purpose of this theoretical essay is met using an inductive top-down theorizing method, whose raw data are the results of an integrated literature review done by searching the EBSCO database using meta keywords describing or explaining each research question related to the Problem Statement. Such a mixed methodology (i.e., integrative literature review and inductive top-down theorizing) allows one to narrow the field of research and leads to a more complete methodology of research with the aim of establishing a new organizational theory. Furthermore, the assumptions and boundary conditions of this method for grounding theory from literature are aligned with one of the key issues of this theoretical essay, which relies on perceptions (i.e., sensory representations) and consequently, on a theory of perception for which attention focus is central.

Inductive Top-Down Theorizing Interest

Inductive top-down theorizing is a mode of theorizing coined by Shepherd and Sutcliffe (2011) that may enhance the discovery or creation of a paradox (within or across paradigms) and is especially appropriate when the body of previous research is vast, dynamic, complex, and/or from disparate sources. Inductive top-down theorizing is most appropriate for understanding and resolving paradoxes that exist in bodies of literature that are extensive and difficult for any one researcher to "know" at any one point in time.

Inductive Top-Down Theorizing Process

During the process of inductive top-down theorizing, the theorist discovers a problem in the literature—tension, opposition, or contradiction among divergent perspectives and explanations of the same phenomenon—and then sets out proposals to create a solution to that problem. Literature (e.g., articles, books, reviews) as data is considered as the truth as it is known today, and during the process of reading, attention focus is central for constructing a limited and temporary coherence field to form, from either author prior knowledge or existing literature, a gist (i.e., Gestalt-like) related to the nature of the phenomenon. Then, following the development of sensory representations, the theorist develops conceptual representations as tentative solutions to the problem.

The constant comparison process helps explain how a conceptual representation develops from bidirectional interaction with sensory representations of the literature, which is facilitated by using dedicated tools (e.g., thought experiments, metaphorical reasoning, or others) while allowing testing of the "fit" of the emerging conceptualization. Shepherd and Sutcliffe (2011) noted that while thought experiments refer to thoughts trials and abstract hypothetical scenarios, metaphorical reasoning provides an openness of meanings.

Theoretical Framework

Theorizing Method

While reading, sensory representations (i.e., perceptions) and conceptual representations were formed and constantly compared to the contextual knowledge of the author. Progressively, by shaking thoughts coming from both sources (i.e., literature and the author's prior knowledge) through a constant comparison process, new theoretical proposals emerged.

Prior Knowledge

Prior knowledge of the author is mainly a result of his education, personal thoughts, and life experience:

- Education is peer heritage used by the author as a landmark.
- Life experience constitutes the meta-context of the author.
- Personal thoughts are the results of life experience filtered through education.

A part of prior author knowledge allows forming the first *gists* that are holistic representations of the environment that does not require attention to stabilize a subset of environmental stimuli, which highlights a lot of potential *bias* of the research study.

Categorization

From the author's perspective, to perceive is to receive and categorize (i.e., doing an interpretation). To receive mobilizes attention from the outside to inside of the self. To categorize is to evaluate and classify a distance from a landmark. This is the way that the author thinks that human beings perceive their environments. Perceptions are realities of the perceivers, while interpretations of these perceptions (i.e., giving meanings to realities) are decisions, which constitute human rationality. Therefore, human rationality and managing of change are two inseparable concepts. The rationality of human beings is built for managing change permanently mainly due to flexibility and the central role of attention, and because contexts and behaviors are changing all the time, interpretations change over time, which highlights the prominent role that attention plays in organizations, which has been perfectly summarized by Jacques Orvain:

> Since the seminal work of Simon (1983), several theoretical frameworks have attention at the heart of their research (Gavetti, Levinthal, & Ocasio, 2007). Three research streams have changed the issue of structuring attention in organizations (Ocasio, 1997). The first endeavored to show how attention could be distributed in the organization (Cyert, 1992); the second how some action scripts allow to develop a particular pattern of mobilization of the attention that has been described as the "Mindfulness" (Weick & Sutcliffe, 2003); the third, called "ABV" (Warning Based View of the firm), has made the study of the role of attention in activities the heart of its approach. (Orvain, 2014, p. 346)

Thus, the study of decision (e.g., theories of choice) with more or less uncertainty (e.g., prospect theory), which precedes most human behaviors, leads to a question on how attention as an antecedent of human rationality proceeds using norms (i.e., shared landmarks), while change occurs over time.

Norms

Norms are shared landmarks, but all shared landmarks do not necessarily become norms. That is a matter of percentage of replication in a group of people. Such replication is precisely the result of attention. Replication means that attention is drawn by what others are doing. Therefore, without attention, no replication is possible, and without replication no norm can exist. Thus, norms are sets of recommendations, which are reinforced through the practice of people who agree to put in practice such recommendations (e.g., communities of practice (COP) are driven by shared norms). Norms have functions (e.g., social, quality, identity), which help to achieve either some expectations (e.g., individual or collective) or a well-identified goal (e.g., regulation, welfare, loyalty), all built within conditional preferences for following behavioral rules that constitute social interactions. Nevertheless, the principal role of norms is to be used as landmarks to assess our environments for making decisions.

Decision-Making

Decision-making (i.e., human rationality) seems to be something personal, a personal act, but, in fact, such an act is always done, according to a context. This concept of context generally refers to the surroundings associated with phenomena, which are typically factors associated with units of analysis that are investigated. On the other hand, the environments can be defined as situational opportunities and constraints that affect the occurrence and meaning of organizational behavior as well as functional relationships between variables. Therefore, one cannot separate an act from the context in which it happens, regardless of the way one considers or characterizes this act (e.g., thinking or doing something else), and this basic process of acting of human beings is true whatever the environment is—open or closed—and whatever the way such a process is managed with more or less paradox embedded. Moreover, although the basic mechanisms of functioning are the same for all human beings (e.g., human rationality), each of us is unique. Such uniqueness is not only expressed via the shape of our body (e.g., visage, fingerprint) but also through the ways we behave facing the world that we are in (e.g., acting, thinking).

Thus, each of us has a unique identity, behavioral style, and motivations. So, considering Banfield's (1958) argument that how men do behave and how they should behave are different matters (p. 129), a dilemma remains unsolved: do we need to think for acting or is thinking an act? While orthodoxy refers to human thoughts (i.e., thinking), orthopraxis refers to human acts (i.e., doing something); nevertheless, both are human behaviors, which have to be more or less in line with social norms (e.g., human knowledge, ethics) like rituals (e.g., civil laws, religion). In this paradigm, building concepts (i.e., thinking) is an allopoietic phenomenon using landmarks (e.g., words or other existing concepts).

By contrast, building meanings is an autopoietic phenomenon that needs *consensus* between at least two people and that requires a tacit common agreement and repetition to exist (e.g., scientific methodology). Therefore, without landmarks (e.g., norms), one cannot think. In the same manner that acting needs landmarks and energy to proceed, the act of thinking needs landmarks and consumes energy. That process, which is run by human rationality, is called interpretation (i.e., a mix of emotional and verbal categorization).

Rationality

Today, we know that human rationality is a mix of emotional intelligence (EI) and verbal intelligence (VI). EI develops first, then language comes along, and VI constructs itself on and with emotions. Emotions come from our sensations, which, for newborns, are the basic means to discover their respective environments (i.e., contexts they are in). Since the time of being in the uterus, the variety of stimuli arriving to our senses are analyzed through a PCM based on pleasure/displeasure, which contributes to shaping our sensibility to perceive, while building our own scale and table of sensations used as landmarks for building our perceptions. Then, progressively, the use of words (i.e., shared norms) helps us to engage in a reflexive interpretation that transforms these sensations into feelings, and the contextual management of their associations (i.e., sensations & feelings) leads to achieving more or less consciously over time the building of our respective and unique rationalities.

Thus, consciousness can be defined as a reflexive process—perceiving one's own perceptions—while introducing the concept of FoC, which introduces non-linear thinking.

Moreover, in this theoretical essay, the author has considered that:

- All human concepts are more or less consciously constructed, and some became more or less shared norms for a group of them (e.g., meanings of words are shared norms), and consciousness is a reflexive process of attention: perceiving one's own perceptions.
- Most human behaviors are more or less distant from shared norms (e.g., social capital), which determine how people are integrated or not into a group of people. That distance allows the introduction of a metric, which explains what people call deviance or abnormality of behavior compared to normal behavior (i.e., accepted norms) in society.
- Norms are shared landmarks, but all shared landmarks do not necessarily become norms. That is a matter of percentage of replication in a group of people (e.g., communities of practice); therefore, what makes a norm depends mostly on the number of people who refer to it, more or less consciously, for acting. Consequently, throughout this theoretical essay, the human being is considered as the *Point of Origin* of the context in which and from which they are taking basic decisions (e.g., acting).

Bibliography

Banfield, E. C. (1958). *The moral basis of a backward society*. New York: Free Press.

Orvain, J. (2014). Le qui-vive organisationnel: Une forme de structuration du lien attention-action. *Management*, *17*(5), 346–370.

Shepherd, D. A., & Sutcliffe, K. M. (2011). Inductive top-down theorizing: A source of new theories of organization. *Academy of Management Review*, *36*(2), 361–380.

5 Findings

The main issue of this theoretical essay is to gain a better understanding of the interactions among OJ, EPJ, and MPJ during OC. Therefore, there is a need to get a deeper understanding of the basic social mechanisms that produce shared norms (e.g., norms of justice), and to examine to what extent the perceptions (e.g., fairness) of such norms experienced by people induce their decision-making (e.g., acceptance, resistance, or neutral) while various levels of change take place over time in organizations. By contrast, the issue is not to formulate what is good or bad (e.g., fair or unfair) from an ethical point of view while managing change, but to provide new insights into what to do for successful OC.

Presentation of the Findings

For each finding, some dedicated gists (i.e., Gestalt-like) have emerged due to the use of the methodology of Shepherd and Sutcliffe (2011). A gist is the result of the holistic representation of the environment that does not require attention to stabilize a subset of the environmental stimuli, which in this study comes from the reading of literature. Moreover, to hold in mind sensory representations over an extended period requires that the author relies on a system other than attention—a system based on beliefs, which have been exposed as *theoretical prolegomena*. Therefore, each of these gists emerged from a process modeled in Figure 5.1.

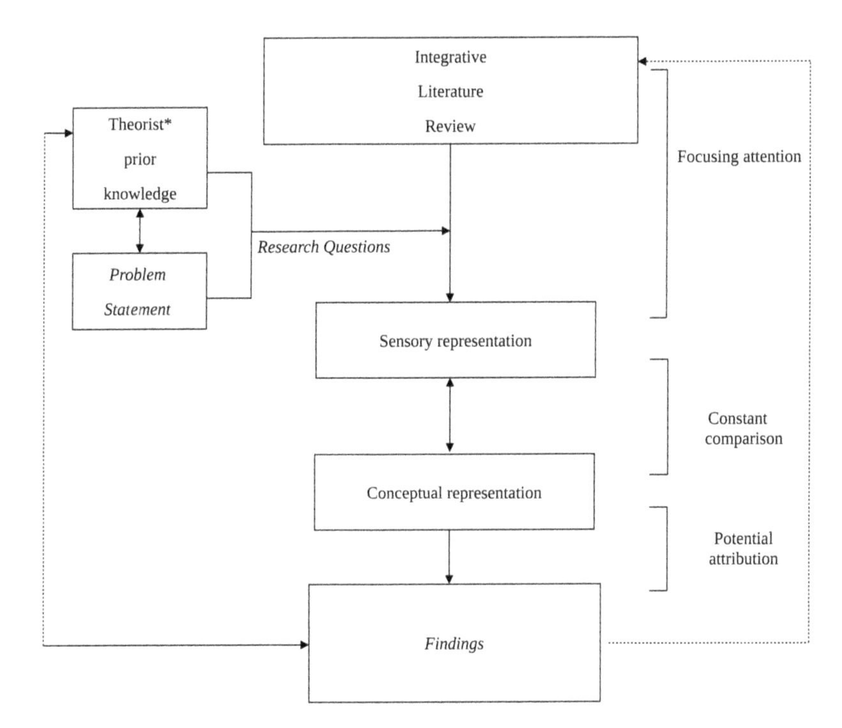

Figure 5.1 Model derived from the original skeleton of Shepherd and Sutcliffe (2011)

Then, in accordance with Shepherd and Sutcliffe's citation (p. 372), metaphors provide sources of analogous information. Therefore, constant comparison through experiments, metaphorical reasoning, or other tools like brainstorming allows testing of the fit of an emerging conceptualization with the theorist's sensory representations to determine the extent of the gap between the two, and provides the basis for bringing the conceptual and sensory representations "into line". The greater the mismatch, the more likely it will trigger further theorizing.

Thus, one can generalize the process stated in Figure 5.1 into an emerging *transitional model* as described in Figure 5.2.

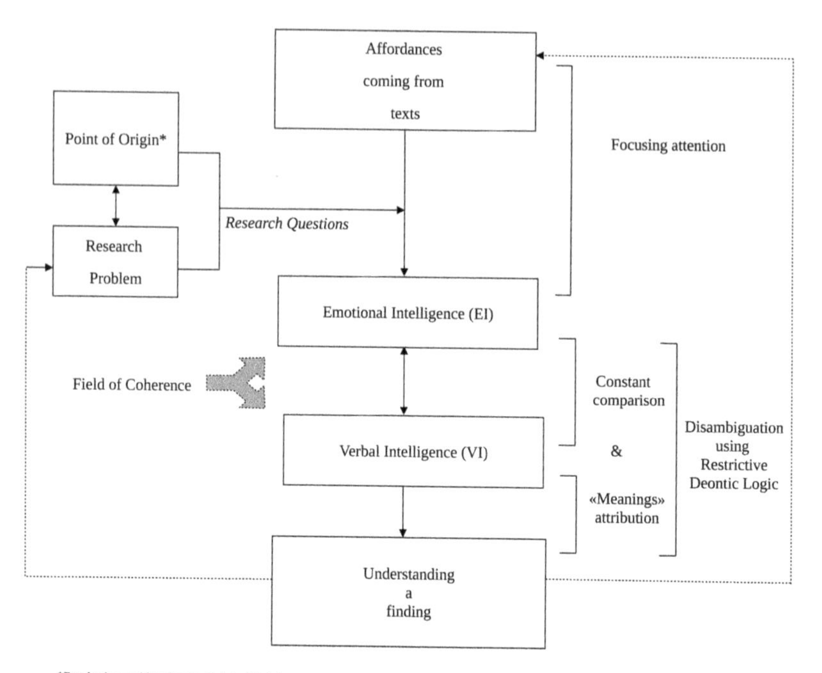

Figure 5.2 How do texts and readers interact while finding takes place?

Thus, while using appropriate data coming from both sources (i.e., the literature and author's prior knowledge), due to coherence theory, the author makes inferences in order to tie the data into a coherent mental representation that he can use to explain the phenomenon. This involves an iterative process of the cognitive system, where incoherent representations are replaced by increasingly more coherent representations. Moreover, the movement toward coherence is bidirectional—the sensory image of the data informs the conceptual representation, and the conceptual representation informs the conception of sensory representation. Therefore, applying the above model to Rensink (2002) allows the following (Figure 5.3).

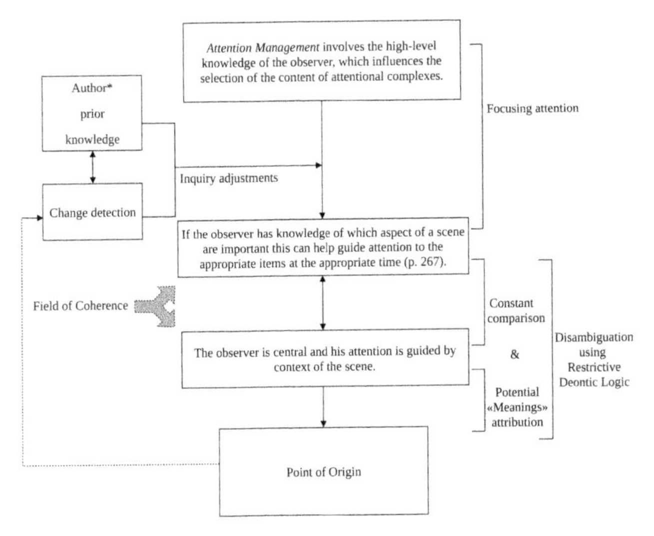

Figure 5.3 Process results described in Figure 5.1 when reading of Rensink's conceptual proposals (2002)

By doing a simple replication, one can get another sample (e.g., Singer, 2015) to produce Figure 5.4, which is related to findings coming from Singer (2015).

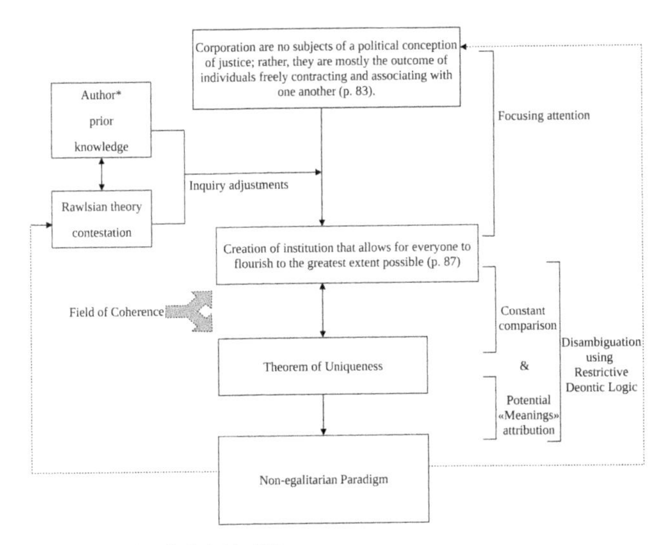

Figure 5.4 Process results described in Figure 5.1 when reading of Singer's conceptual proposals (2015)

Such modeling can be generalized by using each author of Table 5.1.

Table 5.1 An overview of significant sensory representations and potential contribution to theoretical proposal

Topic	*Study*	*Principal Theoretical Contributions*
Attention	Kahneman (1973)	Attention is limited, but the limit is variable from moment to moment. Attention is divisible, and allocation of attention is a matter of degree. Attention is selective and controllable to facilitate the processing of selecting perceptual units.
	Occasio (1997)	Attention of decision-maker shapes organization of the firm, which influences the selection of the content of attentional complexes.
Change detection	Rensink (2002)	Attentional management involves the high-level knowledge of the observer.
Field of coherence	Ravatin (2008)	The human being when he thinks is related to a coherent field. Humans were put in a cage where they frolic, but most of them do not know the existence of this cage.
Affordances	Gibson (1979, 1988)	The medium, substances, surfaces, objects, places, and other animals have affordances for a given animal. They offer benefit or injury, life or death. This is why they need to be perceived.
Theory of action	Von Mises (1949)	Human activity is one arrangement by which the change occurs.
Context	Johns (2006)	Context as a shaper of meaning. Context as a configuration or bundle of stimuli.
Deontic logic	Von Wright (1951, 1968)	Deontic propositions are sometimes, or perhaps always, relative to some so-called moral code. What is obligatory within one moral code may be forbidden within another.
Ternary logic	Arpasi (2003)	A brief introduction to ternary logic.
Rationality unknowns	Neisser, et al. (1996)	Every individual has a biological as well as a social environment that begins in the womb and extends throughout life.
Equality vs. Inequality	Sen (1992)	Deep analysis of equality and inequality into an egalitarian paradigm.
Rawl's contestation	Singer (2015)	John Rawls' theory of justice cannot be applied effectively to a question of business ethics and corporate governance.
Distributive justice	Wang, et al. (2010)	Promoting the same treatment to similar employees and different treatment to different employees.

Then, constant comparison between such representations coming from the literature with the author's prior knowledge (e.g., theoretical prolegomena) allows the identification of some needs.

Need to Establish a Continuum between Behaviors and Contexts

The first important finding from the literature is related to context (i.e., *the world around us*), and experiences that one can experiment with inside it (e.g., *understanding change*), as Rensink said, "the way we experience the world around us" (p. 267). Therefore, one can define that understanding change is to understand the way we experience the world around us.

Moreover, there is a structural gap between any human perceptions (i.e., *understanding the world around us*), just because of the uniqueness of each human being and the unicity of the context in which they exist. Whatever the context is, except for him- or herself being considered as *Point of Origin*, a human being can consider that all material (e.g., things or living beings) or all immaterial (e.g., ideas, practices, events) components around him- or herself constitute a set of affordances generated by this context. This means that each component can be defined by what he or she offers as a set of opportunities of experiences (i.e., *the way we experience the world around us*) toward this human being considered as a Point of Origin. This approach allows the application of Gibson's (1979) concept of affordance to contexts, while each human being can be considered as a Point of Origin of the context in which and from which they are taking basic decisions for doing something (e.g., thinking, speaking, or acting) or nothing.

Then, holding in mind the above conceptual representation, one has to remember the observation that follows: interactions between OJ and MPJ have not yet been precisely examined, mainly because there is a lack of clear understanding of how contexts and behaviors interact dynamically.

Thus, the comparison of the conceptual representation with the above observation leads to examining whether a *continuum* exists between a human being and the context (i.e., a set of affordances) in which they are considered as a Point of Origin. This question has an immediate answer. In the same way that it is possible to break down any context using Gibson's affordances, it is possible to consider a human being as a set of behaviors. Consequently, as soon as one becomes able to construct a continuum between human behaviors and affordances of contexts, one will succeed to manage both dynamically.

This continuum is the golden key for getting a better *understanding of understanding* some unknowns about how human rationality works whatsoever for doing mathematics (Michener, 1978) or for theorizing, while such above recommendations provide a theoretical foundation for better describing and explaining how behaviors and contexts interact while reducing organizational complexity (Lissack & Letiche, 2002), which constitutes a grand challenge.

Need to Integrate a Non-Egalitarian Paradigm while Reasoning

The most important finding coming from the literature is, surprisingly, that none of the organizational scholars will discuss the reality of the concept of equality radically. Therefore, the author concludes that among scholars, there is more or less a consensus of reasoning within the egalitarian paradigm, in which equality of treatment is a key to promote equality, trust, and fairness, while norms of justice (e.g., fairness) are most of the time based on reciprocity (i.e., social expression of equality).

Or, *equality* (i.e., =) is only a convention (i.e., an artifact) that became a habit of human beings, mainly because it allows their rationality to categorize. Then, progressively this habit has been transformed into a belief (i.e., social artifact) that is useful (e.g., calculus) but false, which introduces many *biases* in real life—and, particularly into current norms of justice that are mainly based on the principle of reciprocity, which is the social expression of this well-established *social belief* named equality. Mainly because, most of the time, their attention is not able to go far away from such a strange attractor that represents the concept of equality, most scholars purely and simply ignore the Paradox of Fairness. Consequently, people try to reach objectives that are impossible to reach with equality utopia. Their attention is not able to go away from such a false truth.

Such above collective *selbstverblendung* (i.e., incomprehensible blindness) highlights the limitation of human FoC where lineal and non-lineal landmarks coexist, and the subtle confusion into which many reasonings fall and fail to describe and explain why some challenges already mentioned are today so difficult to overcome (e.g., managing change, justice, or big data), and indeed why such challenges are associated with complexity. Due to the fact that current norms of justice are mainly based on the principle of reciprocity, which is the social expression of that human artifact (i.e., a social belief) named equality, a hypothesis of faulty norms of justice is open, particularly when such norms are used for corporate governance, and nothing is using questions such as "equality of what?" or "why equality?", particularly when examining social issues. Thus, the political consequences (i.e., ends, ways, and means to organize human beings) of the above artifact (i.e., =), which is always false in real life, must be examined thoroughly by organizational scholars due to huge consequences for human organizations.

Need to Introduce New Theoretical Tools for Organizational Research

Like the Point of Origin or the Paradox of Fairness, there is a need to introduce new tools inside the body of knowledge in order to improve the ability of scholars to analyze phenomena using different perspectives (i.e., critical thinking). Applying *affordance theory to contexts* while using restricted deontic logic is a useful process to dig out basic relations between human beings and their environments.

Evaluation of the Findings

Theorem of Uniqueness

$$\forall x, \nexists y \,/\, x = y$$

Everybody knows more or less intuitively or by learning the above statement but forgets, while only keeping it in mind as a truth, this social belief named equality. Nevertheless, for those who believe that the above is a false or a provocative fiction, let's say the following: assuming that equality (i.e., =) is true, then, as each of us called H is a combination of emotional and verbal experiences, we can write $\mathrm{H} = \mathrm{E} + \mathrm{V}$ and whatever H and H′, we have $\mathrm{H} - \mathrm{H}' > 0$ or $\mathrm{H} - \mathrm{H}' < 0$, human beings are different and experience different contexts, so, each time, I add something equal to H and H′, the result is $(\mathrm{H} + \mathrm{X}) - (\mathrm{H}' + \mathrm{X}) > 0$ or $(\mathrm{H} + X) - (\mathrm{H}' + X) < 0$, which demonstrates it is not possible to reduce inequality between H and H′ by treating H and H′ in the same manner (i.e., adding the same X)—one has to add a different X to H and Y to H′ with the aim to reduce the difference between H and H′ with $X - Y = \mathrm{H}' - \mathrm{H}$, and if not, then the inequality will be maintained and most of the time reinforced and not balanced. As Wells (1891) stated: All being is unique, or, nothing is strictly like anything else.

Paradox of Fairness

Most of the time, due to educational norms that promote equality as a truth, human attention is not able to go far away from such a strange attractor that is commonly shared (i.e., shared norms). Consequently, instead of finding a solution according to the reality of inequality, people pursue objectives that are impossible to reach through equal treatment. Their attention is not able to go away from such a false truth. They are convinced that administering different treatments means an unequal position that is prohibited most of the time for moral considerations. They have been trained by education and forced by their environment (i.e., a paradigm) to consider that equality exists as a tangible fact in which they must trust.

Point of Origin

Although such a convention (i.e., Point of Origin) seems very simple or a "naive" concept, it is in fact a very powerful key to separate contexts, which is a must for understanding more complex concepts that one needs to use for better describing and explaining human behavior and its antecedents, which are *understanding* before *decision-making* (i.e., verbal intelligence). In this way, all of *what* (i.e., an opportunity for doing something with) is around us as a *Point of Origin* is an opportunity for an experiment. Then, one decides to experiment or not with that *what*—which means accepting or rejecting that opportunity for acting. Therefore, the meaning of doing/acting something is as much informative as that of doing/acting nothing.

Although such a concept is original (i.e., a thought experiment of the author) as indicated in Table 5.1, some useful references coming from the literature highlight such Point of Origin (Gibson, 1979; Kahneman, 1973; Ocasio, 1997; Ravatin, 2008; Rensink, 2002; Von Wright, 1951). Of course, such a list is not exhaustive.

Affordance Applied to Contexts

Offering opportunities of experiments is precisely what affordance means, when defining the concept of affordance itself. Therefore, any context can be considered as a set of opportunities (i.e., a set of potential experiments) of doing or not doing something due to the affordances related to that context. This approach allows a systemic desegmentation of any context (i.e., the environment of a Point of Origin), whatever its components (i.e., material or immaterial), and means visual, perceptual, or conceptual, which contributes to reducing the complexity of understanding any organizational complexity.

Restricted Deontic Logic

Restricted Deontic Logic using a ternary logic instead of quaternary logic comes with the idea that ancients (i.e., early human beings on Earth) had first the need to survive their environment. Such a basic need to "survive" is probably one of the basic experiments that a human being had to do and observe around him or her. What I must do to survive leads to basic conceptual representation of *obligation*, while what I don't do in order to still be alive leads to the *forbidden* concept.

Then, progressively, navigating between these two nascent basic concepts of obligation and forbidden (i.e., what one must do or not in order to survive) leads to the construction of sensory representations and verbal conceptions of an archaic ternary logic that was only related to the fact to be or not be alive. The third element (i.e., undetermined) was a negative deduction of the first two, meaning that I don't know yet if that experiment was an obligation or a forbidden for surviving. Thus, facing some new danger or just while discovering their environment (i.e., various contexts), most of the time human beings don't know if they are facing an obligation or a forbidden until the act itself reveals the consequence (i.e., death or still alive). Therefore, I consider that declining deontic logic into a ternary choice (e.g., obligatory, forbidden, or undetermined) is conceivable. Furthermore, the logical system of decision-making that has underpinned the decisions of the behaviors that human beings must do or must not do in order to survive is a good start to imagine how human beings have more or less consciously constructed a basic process to make choices (i.e., a basic mechanism of decision-making), which they have learned for survival in the early stages of humanity.

Bibliography

Arpasi, J. P. (2003). A brief introduction to ternary logic. Retrieved from http://aymara.org/ternary/ternary.pdf

Gibson, E. J. (1988). Exploratory behavior in the development of perceiving, acting, and the acquiring of knowledge. *Annual Review of Psychology*, *39*(1), 1–41.

Gibson, J. J. (1979). *The ecological approach to visual perception*. Boston, MA: Houghton Mifflin.

Johns, G. (2006). The essential impact of context on organizational behavior. *Academy of Management Review*, *31*(2), 386–408.

Kahneman, D. (1973). *Attention and effort*. Englewood Cliffs, NJ: Prentice–Hall Inc.

Letiche, H., Lissack, M., & Schultz, R. (2011). *Coherence in the midst of complexity: Advance in social complexity theory*. Hampshire: Palgrave Macmillan.

Lissack, M. R., & Letiche, H. (2002). Complexity, emergence, resilience, and coherence: gaining perspective on organizations and their study. *Emergence*, *4*(3), 72–94.

Michener, E. R. (1978). Understanding understanding mathematics. *Cognitive Sciences*, *2*(4), 361–383.

Neisser, U., Boodoo, G., Bouchard, T. J., Boykin, A. W., Brody, N., Ceci, S. J., & Urbina, S. (1996). Intelligence: Knowns and unknowns. *The American Psychological Association, Inc.*, *51*(2), 77–101.

Ocasio, W. (1997). Towards an attention–based view of the firm. *Strategic Management Journal*, *18*(1), 187–206.

Ravatin, J. (2008). *Développements autour des champs de cohérence*. Tome I, 1ère et 2ème partie. Lyon: Editions du Cosmogone.

Rensink, R. A. (2002). Change detection. *Annual Review of Psychology*, *53*, 245–277.

Sen, A. K. (1992). *Inequality reexamined*. Cambridge, MA: Harvard University Press.

Shepherd, D. A., & Sutcliffe, K. M. (2011). Inductive top-down theorizing: A source of new theories of organization. *Academy of Management Review*, *36*(2), 361–380.

Singer, A. (2015). There is no Rawlsian theory of corporate governance. *Business Ethics Quarterly*, *25*(1), 65–92.

Von Mises, L. (1949, ed. 1985). *L'action humaine: Traité d'économie*. Paris: Presses Universitaires de France (P.U.F).

Von Wright, G. H. (1951, ed. 2007). Deontic logic. *Mind, New Series*, *60*(237), 1–15.

Von Wright, G. H. (1968). An essay in deontic logic and the general theory of action. *Acta Philosophica Fennica*, *21*, 1–55.

Wang, S., Liao, J., Xia, D., & Chang, T. (2010). The impact of organizational justice on work performance: Mediating effects of organizational commitment and leader-member exchange. *International Journal of Manpower*, *31*(6), 660–677.

Wells, H. G. (1891). The rediscovery of the unique. *Fortnightly Review*, 50 (July 1891), 106–111.

6 Outcomes

Considering that it is crucial for developing theories allowing organizations to get practical outcomes during periods of change, organizational scholars have called for a more dynamic conceptualization of OJ in the workplace, and a better understanding of perceptions of justice. Nevertheless, despite many theories or practical approaches to OC, successful OC remains elusive, which may explain the poor success rate of change programs in general, whose failures sometimes have catastrophic consequences, while change initiatives are among the most important projects an organization can undertake to gain competitive advantage. Therefore, the purpose of this theoretical essay was, first, to introduce some new concepts (e.g., the Paradox of Fairness) resulting from a non-egalitarian paradigm, in order to get a better understanding of the interactions among OJ, EPJ, and MPJ during OC, while providing new theoretical tools (e.g., Point of Origin) or highlighting existing theories that have not yet been fully exploited (e.g., Gibson's affordances, deontic logic). Thus, the purpose of this theoretical essay has been met using an inductive top-down theorizing method, whose raw data have been the results of an integrated literature review done by searching the EBSCO database using meta keywords describing each research question related to the Problem Statement. While the non-egalitarian paradigm shift that has been done can meet resistances due to the habits of human beings as a result of the shared norms currently related to the equality convention, the main delimitation of this theoretical essay is that the literature has been voluntarily restricted (i.e., filtered), and consequently does not take into account all human knowledge regarding the phenomenon under investigation. Moreover, the prior knowledge of the author (e.g., theoretical prolegomena) brings a lot of bias that can be criticized.

Significant Outcomes

The main theoretical and practical outcome of this theoretical essay is that for reducing inequalities, instead of proceeding by equal treatment, it is necessary and preferable to promote differentiated treatments in the process of distributive justice. Thus, one can model the response to the CRQ by completing the skeleton of Shepherd and Sutcliffe (2011), as in Figure 6.1.

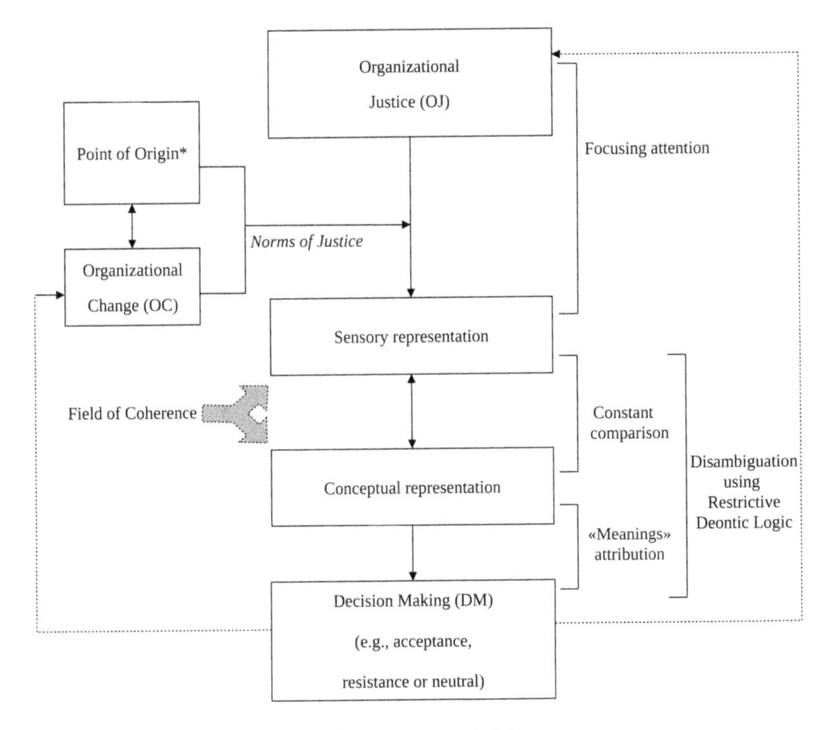

Figure 6.1 How are norms of justice, perceptions of these norms, and decisions related to these perceptions interwoven when people assess change and justice in organizations?

This model allows delivery of an immediate response to SRQ2 by using metaphorical reasoning as follows (Figure 6.2).

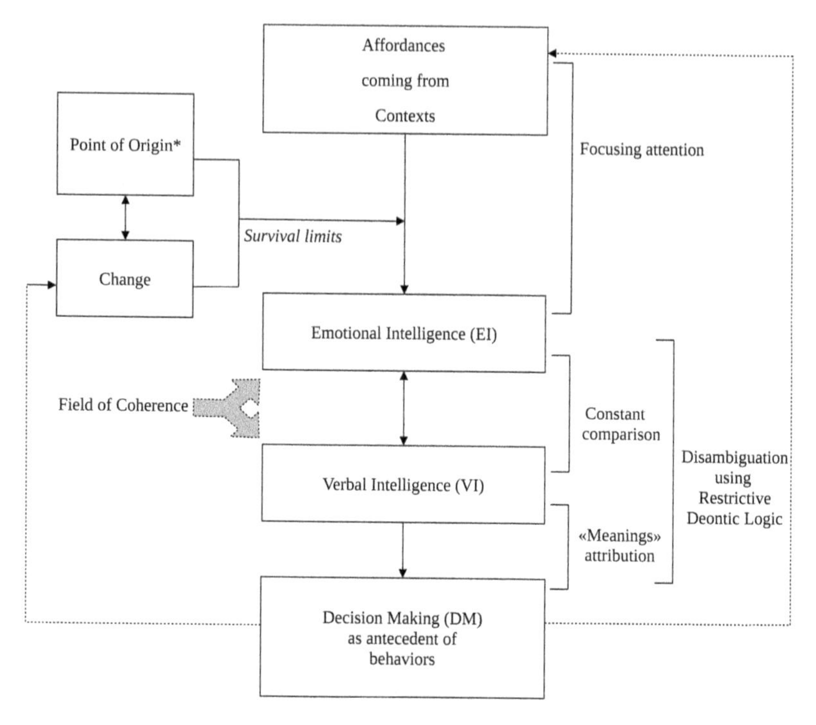

Figure 6.2 How do contexts and behaviors interact while change takes place?

While keeping in mind the Theorem of Uniqueness, the appropriate use of the Point of Origin, the Affordances Applied to Contexts, and the Restricted Deontic Logic to human behaviors, all together lead to a better understanding of how contexts and behaviors interact.

Finally, for responding to SRQ1, the answer is given by the following two models, depending on whether you are a manager or an employee, as it is described in Figures 6.3 and 6.4.

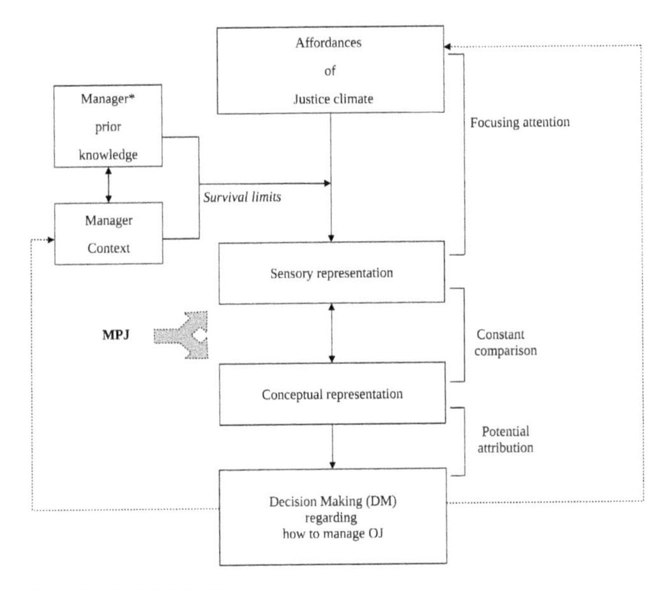

Figure 6.3 How to improve Organizational Justice (OJ) during Orgnizational Change (OC): from the manager's perspective?

And the difference is about the outcome of the evaluation process (i.e., understanding).

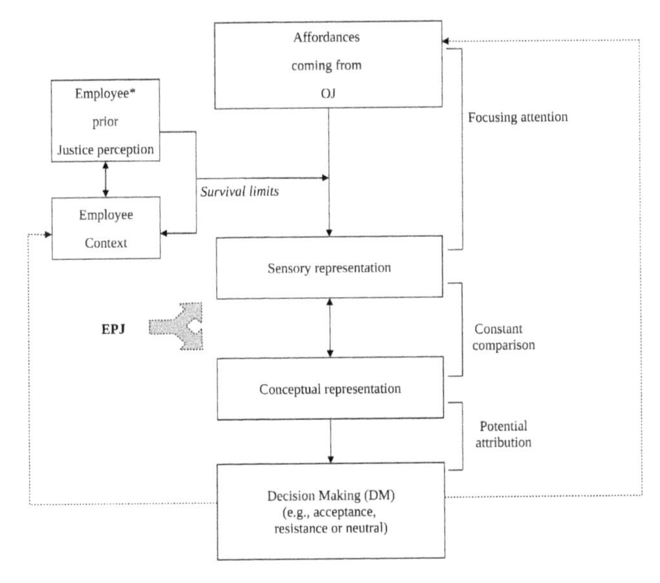

Figure 6.4 How to improve OJ during OC: from the employee's perspective?

Implications for Theory

Promoting Distributive Justice while Administering Differentiated Treatments

Given that the main theoretical and practical outcome of this research study is that for reducing inequalities, instead of proceeding by equal treatment, it is necessary and preferable to promote differentiated treatments in the process of distributive justice, this fundamental finding has huge consequences for all human organizations. In other words, although the concept of equality is a useful convention (i.e., human artifact), and a symbolic simplification for doing maths (e.g., calculus), equality cannot be applicable to living beings and socially promoting equality is an error. Therefore, promoting constantly and most often in rhyme equality is nonsense.

Instead, recognition of the Theorem of Uniqueness allows understanding more deeply why it is so important to care for each other. Although sometimes two people can think or behave in the same way, they are not identical, and this is precisely because each human being is a unique personality, that we, the others, must take care in various ways, respecting their own differences instead of trying to normalize them. Thus, promoting distributive justice by administering differentiated treatments is more appropriate in the attempt to compensate for our differences. In other words, the fact that each element is unique means that we must take care of it precisely because it is unique. Then, the Point of Origin leads to managing affordance coming from the deconstruction of the environments, while Restricted Deontic Logic provides rules for managing such deconstruction. Thus, what appears complex to manage becomes simple, and a lot of consequences, both theoretical and practical, are attached to that process. Furthermore, as soon as one is able to identify what is the continuum that links contexts, as they are newly defined, and human behaviors, a new *understanding of understanding* will emerge with many applications (e.g., smart computers) for the benefit of all humanity.

Delivering Differentiated Treatments while Elevating Human Dignity

Another major outcome that derives immediately from the Theorem of Uniqueness is related to the concept of double-unicity, defined as follows: whatever element you may consider, as there is no other element equal to it, due to this uniqueness, this element is a part of something bigger that forms a unity, which is itself unique. Fromm (1956) had already pointed out this idea of unicity when examining what equality meant in a religious context, highlighting that each one of us is a unique entity (i.e., not duplicable entity), while we are all one (p. 52). Furthermore, considering that contemporary capitalistic society had transformed the original religious meaning of equality to the equality of automatons, of men who have lost their individuality, he added that today equality means "sameness" rather than "oneness" (p. 14). Then he concluded that just as modern mass production requires the standardization of commodities, so the social process requires standardization of man, and this standardization is called equality (p. 15), while the individual is introduced into the conformity pattern at the age of three or four, and subsequently never loses his contact with the herd (i.e., herd of conformity for routinization) (p. 16). Thus, the social world created by human beings is or ought to be built, while recognizing these three fundamental principles, which are: hierarchy due to language, asymmetry of information due to uniqueness, and double-unicity as a result. Then, the duty to take care of this *double-unicity* becomes simple, and can be easily appropriated by human beings as a universal landmark (i.e., a shared norm, whatever the cultural expression of human beings). Thenceforth, each human being has the right and the duty to care of himself, to care for the set constituted by himself as Point of Origin and the context around him, including all other living beings or the other things that are inside (i.e., personal ecosystem).

This duty of "care" mentioned above corresponds to the first of the four elements mentioned by Fromm (1956), placing "the art of loving" and "love" as a central issue of management for the future to come. Instead of Freud's assumption, Fromm understood that all human behaviors could not be only related to sexual frustrations, while highlighting four mutually interdependent elements common to all forms of love, which are: care, respect, responsibility, and knowledge. Such a definition helps the author to separate at work what the author calls rational love from emotional love with or without sexual desires or religious considerations. Thus, considering rational love (RL) as an interpersonal creative capacity rather than an emotion (i.e., emotional love) has huge consequences, because at work it avoids confusion in human minds within their relations with others about what is related to libido or not. Therefore, it is possible to love somebody without any sexual intention, like most mothers do every day of their lives with their children. For sure, such an approach of management should be qualified as paternalism, but it is not the case when applying the other three recommendations of Fromm (i.e., respect, responsibility, and knowledge) that constitute all forms of love, which in practice reinforce every manager and not only CEOs, in private or public sectors, to strengthen the competitiveness level of his/her organization using the CR2K guideline of *Managing by Love* as follows:

- *Care* is the ability to grow something or somebody, and the first duty of a manager is to grow the business he or she leads.
- *Respect* is the ability to take people and manage them as they are instead of what they could be. In a world where social exchanges are global across multicultural countries, the ability to accept people as they are is a five-star management standard that international managers have to apply every business day.

- *Responsibility* is the ability to deliver what the other asks from you. This is a common duty of all managers both inside (e.g., mid-management, employees) and outside (e.g., clients, stakeholders) the organization he or she manages.
- *Knowledge* is what that manager seeks to acquire both implicitly and explicitly due to the power attached to information—sometimes with the aim to reduce such asymmetry or sometimes to increase it—always with the aim to take advantage of that knowledge.

Most of the time, the fact that a manager provides differentiated treatments is something that he or she does naturally—but often, with the fear of being accused of favoritism. Therefore, delivering differentiated treatments while having in mind care, respect, responsibility, and knowledge is a good attitude for a manager to reduce inequality, and to get positive perceptions of justice from people under his/her supervision.

Human Dignity Cannot Be Reduced to Ethics or Performance

Although the issue of this research study is not to formulate what is good or bad (e.g., fair or unfair) from an ethical point of view while managing change and justice, but to provide new insights of what to do for succeeding with OC, I would like to add the following few words that need to be attached to the whole study: inside the social construction or social game, lie some values like *ethics* or *performance* (i.e., shared norms), which as landmarks are both ways to measure the distance between human beings between themselves, and also to measure the distance between themselves and nature. Most often, *ethics* is linked with what is *good* or *not*, which is a verbalization of *pleasure/displeasure* (i.e., a conceptual representation of PCM*)*, while *performance* is linked with the level of satisfaction (i.e., pleasure/displeasure), that benefits one or more human beings. Therefore, such concepts (i.e., ethics or performance) are relative and cannot be considered as ends. They are only the means to promote reciprocity in social exchanges, i.e., having the will and ability for doing the best for managing common goods like life, or to promote some universal values like brotherhood, both of which are human duties.

Recommendations for Practice

Improving Distributive Justice by Aligning Perceptions of Justice

Due to the fact that equality is a utopia (i.e., something that cannot be achieved), the only way to succeed with OC is to manage OJ in a manner that aligns as much as possible EPJ and MPJ, and such alignment can only be achieved by a constant dialog between participants (e.g., employees and managers). This result is consistent with what organizational scholars have found and recommend through distributive justice. Such dialog must be done with the aim to find a *consensus* and not to be regulated by *vote*, like people are often used to doing under the banner of democracy.

Of course, it is not enough to gain new theoretical insights without setting up some kind of methodology that helps to apply them in practice. Therefore, in future research, one needs to examine in what manner the management of differentiated treatments can be done without falling into arbitrary decisions. How can one differentiate such differentiated treatments? Who is going to decide what is the best adaptation, and why? How should rational love be managed? How can such a paradigm shift be scaled up for a broader and general implementation? All of these questions need a response.

Aligning Perceptions of Justice Using More Dialog

Most of our relationships in life or in business are based on two principles, asymmetry of information and "hierarchy". The principle of hierarchy comes from language. When we speak, we must organize our speech with a linear form using one "dimension". This means that we must put words in a certain order according to what we have learned at school about grammar, syntactic, and semantic rules. We live in a space with at least three dimensions, with a fourth dimension, which is time. The passage from four dimensions to one dimension is precisely made by using the principle of hierarchy. We must transform descriptions of our environment or of our behaviors, which by definition are in four dimensions, into a series of words put in order in one dimension. That process is the major reason why our societies are built within hierarchies.

Regarding the asymmetry of information, which is highlighted by the Theorem of Uniqueness, such a fact is due to the way we perceive nature. For most individuals, nature is observable. This means that most think as if they are separated from this nature. This is the way they exist. But, this is because this separation is made—that they need to evaluate permanently the difference or the distance between themselves and nature. This is another reason why the asymmetry exists and why such a principle governs most of the relations people have with nature or with living beings around them. This is also the reason why the reduction of the asymmetry of information will bring in the future more consciousness of the hierarchy principle that governs our civilizations. Moreover, one can define the process used by human beings to live in four dimensions and to speak within one dimension as a primary human social mechanism due to the use of natural language, which I call "primary hierarchy".

Then, it is easier to understand why, socially, hierarchies are so present in human organizations. Such social hierarchies can be split into two categories according to either the hierarchy being based on competencies (i.e., hierarchy of competencies) or the hierarchy being based on centers of interests (i.e., hierarchy of center of interest). I suggest considering that the optimum of efficiency of a human commitment at work is obtained when the spread between both hierarchies is the smallest.

Using More Dialog for Reaching Excellence

For reaching excellence and creating value, managers must promote dialog, which contributes to reducing conflict while promoting common understanding (i.e., shared meanings). Doing that, they have an obligation to open their hearts and to develop their understandings. As Jung (1932) said, "Your vision will become clear only when you can look into your own heart. Who looks outside, dreams; who looks inside, awakes".

Therefore, a key to excellence in management is to organize a true participation within constant dialog across people in order to get and manage their commitments. Or, that approach is precisely reinforced by promoting distributive justice using differentiated treatments. Thus, having understood that information is data interpreted by a human being, and that the meaning attached depends on both behaviors and contexts, one becomes able to determine the rules of the function "understand" by linking not only what people say but by managing contexts and behaviors between who is speaking and who is listening. This practice applied in business administration allows some simplifications in the way of managing the "meaning" of all related data that need to be set up in order to succeed with OC.

When carrying out such a practice, it becomes easier to manage communication and cooperation between people working in multicultural organizations, while considering that all parts involved are more characterized by "what they do" instead of by "what they are". This approach of managing the meanings of behaviors in contexts, can integrate multiple variables or risk factors dynamically, and enhance any current tools for doing prospective analysis using a deterministic approach (i.e., with no use of Bayesian maths), which holds a high interest in insurance companies or investments in the banking industry, while managing the fundamentals of risk management, pure finance, or credit scoring.

Reaching Excellence to Promote Dignity

Whatever organizational change is, there are no winners or losers, but just people who generally speaking need to preserve their workplace for their living. Therefore, through constant dialog, the right and duty of any manager is to promote dignity. Moreover, due to the concept of *double-unicity*, who promotes the dignity of the other elevates his own dignity. Thus, while the *Theorem of Uniqueness* draws attention, which is maintained by the Paradox of Fairness, the manager who thinks about the concept of *double-unicity* opens both his mind and his heart (e.g., *Rational Love* (RL)), which allows him to find the right "doing", exactly like Jung stated for getting approval of his plan of change in organizations (i.e., OC). This approach of managing distributive justice while promoting differentiated treatments using RL with its CR2K guideline (i.e., care, respect, responsibility, and knowledge) as a methodology is what the author calls *Managing by Love* (MbL), whose list of concepts is summarized in Table 6.1.

Table 6.1 List of concepts used while theorizing MbL

Concepts	*Outcomes*
Theory of Uniqueness Paradox of Fairness Point of Origin	Differentiated Treatments
Double-Unicity Care Rational Love	Care, Respect, Responsibility, and Knowledge

And, the functioning of which is highlighted by Figure 6.5.

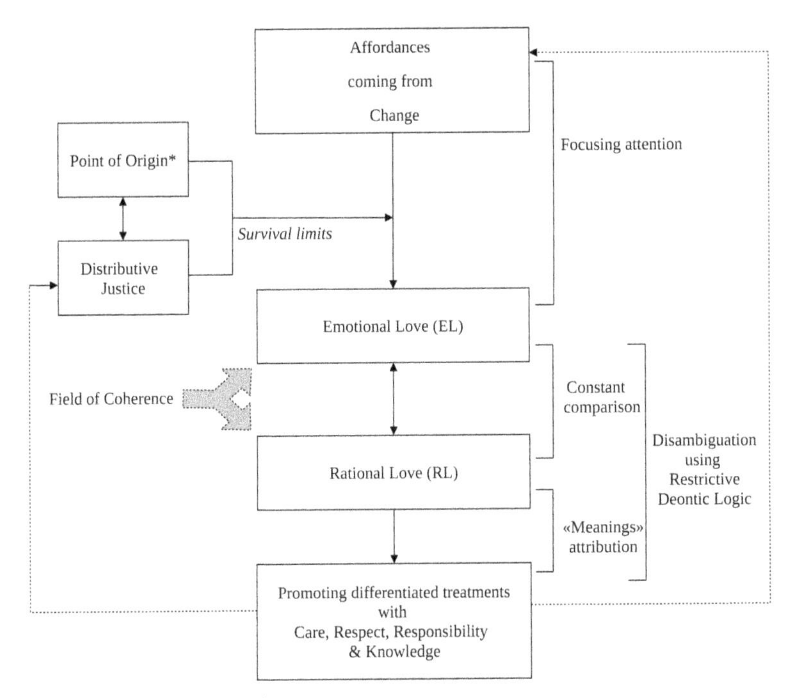

Figure 6.5 Managing by Love (MbL)

While Fromm (1956) considered that the principle underlying capitalistic society and the principle of love are incompatible (p. 121), the above is an attempt to introduce Rational Love (RL) into business administration. Therefore, I hope that such a methodological proposal (i.e., Managing by Love) will be examined thoroughly by scholars and practitioners, while today, most human organizations are facing fear, intolerance, and disputes.

Old and Hot Controversial Topics

To What Extent Rational Love (RL) and Managing by Love (MbL) are Relevant Concepts for Building a Less Unjust Society?

In a nutshell, while politics begins from the conception of the self, justice and social order begin with consideration of the other. Justice or injustice perception depends mostly on how this relationship (i.e., dialog) between self and other is conceptualized and ruled. While assuming that equality exists, it is commonly admitted that as the opposite of arbitrariness, justice requires that where two cases are relevantly alike, they should be treated in the same way. Similarly, when two cases are different, they ought not to be treated alike. Then, a contradiction occurs simply because discrimination (i.e., not provide equal treatment) against someone is often based on an arbitrary selection of traits like race, gender, social origin, or beliefs, which otherwise can always be presented as an absolute deprivation. Thus, it becomes very easy to systematically consider that taking social action on such negative preference (e.g., social deprivation) leads to "bad" or unjust distribution. Therefore, when people are claiming that race, gender, social origin or beliefs should not obstruct anyone for getting social reward according to his/her merit or usefulness (e.g., job, position, diploma ...), these claims make sense only in a context in which race, gender, social origin or beliefs are precisely used to select people. Then, this context leads one to implement corrective action to compensate for this negative preference (e.g., affirmative action). Conversely, MbL is a methodology built within a non-egalitarian paradigm, which enhances dialog for reducing social asymmetry (e.g., inequality) between the self and the other, whatever categorization (i.e., preference) used to account their difference.

For a long time, in practice, justice and fairness have often been in contradiction. Many judges or lawyers experience such difference within their careers. Although both concepts are related to "what is due to others" for aligning conception of social order, justice is the result of enforceable norms of social conduct (i.e., law), while fairness is more oriented with duties, which means "what to be ought to others". Both rights and duties are interrelated with the aim to provide peaceful conflict resolution according to a social order that prevails into society. One is a social external force (i.e., law) that is more or less obtained through voting protocol, while duty is an internal force embedded into cultural tradition, habits, or rituals. Thus, RL as a procedural dialog for taking action with the other helps in practice to better understand rights and duties according to cultural boundaries (e.g., laws, habits, rituals ...). For example, a major criticism of Sen's capabilities approach is that it is not a theory of justice that can guide a distributive model for society. Therefore, equality of resources fails to achieve relational equality because it cannot adequately address discrimination (e.g., positive or negative preference) and other social barriers that might impede individuals from relating to another as equals. Ramanujam, Caivano, and Agnello recently stated that capability theorists have been unable to adequately explain how their approach will be operationalized in practice (2019). Thus, in countries where growth potential has been hindered by deep structural inequalities (e.g., lack of recognition and redistribution) and entrenched social barriers affecting workforce participation (e.g., India), a working theory of distributive justice must contend with the barriers that impede people's participation in social and economic activity. Then, slow-moving and fast-moving institutions can play a decisive role in promoting educational justice that can be enhanced by any procedural justice that provides guidelines for managing inequalities (e.g., MbL).

To What Extent Are RL and MbL Relevant Tools for Educational Justice?

Regarding educational justice, Ruck, Mistry, and Flanagan (2019) point that there is a need in developmental psychology to advance theoretical and empirical knowledge based on children and adolescents' perceptions, experiences, and reasoning about economic inequality, with attention to the processes by which inequality affects developmental outcomes. The gap that youth perceive between the ideal and real levels of inequality in their society has political implications, which is bigger within an unfair society, particularly whether government is unresponsive. Understanding how young people learn about inequality helps to make social change. Therefore, embedded in an instructional design framework, RL should be a useful guideline for teaching young people how to deal with inequalities and justice theories. Thus, coinciding with Sen's recommendation—who is averse to building a well-defined theory of justice but rather prefers to investigate how real-life unjust situations can be turned into more just situations, even if perfect justice is theoretically unattainable—RL and MbL are theoretical proposals that constitute an attempt to manage inequalities for building a less unjust society.

Suggestions for Future Research

Toward a General Theory of Context Management (GTCM)

Looking forward to finding the continuum cited above, another main practical implication of the findings of this research study is to provide a better understanding of how contexts and behaviors interact by combining Gibson's affordance (1979) to contexts and restricted deontic logic (RDL) (i.e., ternary) to behaviors—from the author's perspective, such a combination including the concept of Point of Origin allows researchers, in practice, to move toward establishing a general theory of context management (GTCM) able to better describe and explain how human behaviors and contexts interact dynamically. Potential applications are huge for security (e.g., cybersecurity), while the problem is not the ability to track human behaviors but to understand the meaning of behavior in context.

Then, by simply using metaphorical reasoning instead of *contexts* for managing meanings of *behaviors*, it becomes conceivable to define a *restricted GTCM* applied to *texts* for managing meanings of *words*, which is also a grand challenge of human beings. Once this problem is solved, it becomes possible to achieve smart computers.

Today, for a computer to become really intelligent, the problem to solve is not to manage big data, but to be able to understand the meaning of words in context (i.e., to manage meanings of these words automatically according their particular environments). As soon as this pending problem of Natural Language Processing (NLP) will be solved, then truly smarts personal computers (SPC) will be available on the market ready to disseminate human knowledge at the right time at the right place, whatever the cultures (e.g., languages) or prior knowledge of their users. Nevertheless, such a general theory ruling meanings produced by contexts and behaviors cannot be achieved without having found the right theoretical *continuum* between *contexts* and *behaviors*.This is the reason why, as described in Table 6.2, such a theory (i.e., GTCM) is currently incomplete.

Table 6.2 List of concepts used while theorizing the GTCM

Concepts	*Outcomes*
Theory of Uniqueness	Infinity of Contexts
Paradox of Fairness	Imbrication of Contexts
Point of Origin	Delimitation of Contexts
Affordances of Contexts	Disambiguation of Contexts
Restricted Deontic Logic	Disambiguation of Behaviors
Continuum* between contexts and behaviors	The Missing Link
Incomplete GTCM	

* The golden key mentioned by the author

As previously mentioned, the missing *continuum* is the *golden key*. Therefore, new research must focus on finding this key. As the progress of thoughts (i.e., the body of knowledge) is often the result of deconstruction of widely accepted shared norms (e.g., equality), providing new insight into this issue, which is closely related to the *understanding of understanding*, is still an open grand challenge of human beings, and a small step ahead on this grand challenge is a large step ahead for the whole of humanity.

Conclusions

Most of the new concepts introduced by the author (e.g., *Theorem of Uniqueness*, *Paradox of Fairness*, *Point of Origin*, *Double-Unicity*, *Affordances of Contexts*, and *Restricted Deontic Logic*) come from practice (i.e., observation of the real world), and then have been more or less combined to produce theoretical proposals (e.g., *Managing by Love*) to respond to research questions while providing new orientation for future research (e.g., encourage the discovery of a continuum between contexts and behaviors). Thus, having responded to the three research questions, the author demonstrates that the results of this research correspond with his initial objectives. MbL as a theory is a guideline to enhance managers' ability to succeed with organizational change while providing a distributive justice with the aim to reduce inequality among participants. This management approach can be experimented with by every person who leads a team while enhancing his or her leadership.

By contrast, GTCM is a reasonable attempt to recommend further research for setting up a general theory that allows better description and explanation of how people behave in contexts. Regarding the impact of the assumptions made and any ethical dimensions that need to be considered for the interpretation of the results, there are a lot of biases, mainly due to the prior knowledge of the author (i.e., theoretical prolegomena), which constitute as a whole a barrier for sharing knowledge acquired throughout a life of multidisciplinary research (e.g., creative thinking). Therefore, more effort is needed to disseminate such findings, while at the same time research must be undertaken to complete these first results in order to better highlight how this present contribution can enhance the whole body of human knowledge. Nevertheless, keeping in mind that when facing a new theory the most important thing is to know what can one do concretely with it, from the perspective of the author, some results of this study already constitute a significant contribution to the body of knowledge by providing a better understanding of how human rationality works with the aim of improving the management of justice and change in organizations.

Bibliography

Fromm, E. (1956). *The art of loving*. New York: Harper Perennial.

Gibson, J. J. (1979). *The ecological approach to visual perception*. Boston, MA: Houghton Mifflin.

Jung, C. (1932). *The psychology of Kundalini yoga*. Princeton, NJ: Princeton University Press.

Ramanujam, N., Caivano, N., & Agnello, A. (2019). Distributive justice and the sustainable development goals: Delivering agenda 2030 in India. *Law and Development Review*, *12*(2), 495–536.

Ruck, M. D., Mistry, R. S., & Flanagan, C. A. (2019). Children's and adolescent's understanding and experience of economic inequality: An introduction to the special section. *Developmental Psychology*, *55*(3), 449–456.

Shepherd, D. A., & Sutcliffe, K. M. (2011). Inductive top-down theorizing: A source of new theories of organization. *Academy of Management Review*, *36*(2), 361–380.

Index

Page numbers in **bold** denote tables, those in *italic* denote figures.

www.ingramcontent.com/pod-product-compliance
Ingram Content Group UK Ltd.
Pitfield, Milton Keynes, MK11 3LW, UK
UKHW020426010325
455677UK00029B/1023